LIVING
& DYING

with

PURPOSE AND GRACE

LIVING

DYING

with
PURPOSE AND GRACE

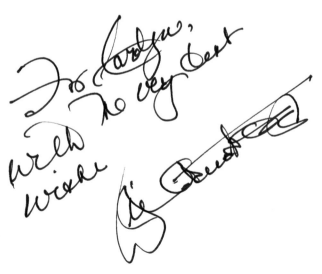

JAMES ARMSTRONG

2010

RIDERGREEN

Rider Green Book Publishers
107 Market Street
Portsmouth, NH 03801

Book and cover design by Jaimie Knapp

Cover art: "Impression, Sunrise" (1872), Claude Monet. Image acquired as a work in the public domain from Awesome Art (www.awesome-art.biz).

Library of Congress Control Number: 2010923109

ISBN 978-0-9819921-1-2

First printing, March, 2010.

This book is printed on recycled, chlorine-free paper and manufactured in the U. S. A. in accordance with environmentally certified production standards.

FOR SHERI,

WHOSE WONDROUSLY CARING,
UNSELFISH LOVE MADE THIS
BOOK POSSIBLE.

TABLE OF CONTENTS

FOREWORD

Long years ago the renowned English essayist Hillaire Belloc arrived at a London auditorium to listen to the lecture of a distinguished British author, only to hear the chairman of the event announce that the speaker had fallen ill and was unable to speak. Upon seeing Belloc in the audience the chairman asked if he would address the audience extemporaneously. "What subject may I address?" Belloc inquired. "Anything except religion or politics," replied the chairman. "Whereupon," said Belloc, "having been barred from discussing the two subjects that most concern mankind, I turned on my heel and departed."

As you will soon discover, Jim Armstrong is not afraid to probe the depths of both religion and politics.

Obviously he has not isolated himself in a cloister, in search of personal sainthood. Rather, he has toiled in a world of sin and virtue, sadness and happiness, skepticism and faith, cruelty and kindness, defeat and glory.

In quoting the ethicist Joseph Fletcher, the author summarized the message of this slim but extremely helpful volume: "Only one thing is intrinsically good, namely love; nothing else at all." Armstrong goes on to say, "Love is not simply something we offer, something we give to another. With the passage of time, if we are moving in the right direction, it infuses all of our actions; it denotes who we are. To love unselfishly, in the relationships of home and family, in the demanding responsibilities of industry and commerce, in the give and take of social action and statecraft, promoting 'the general welfare,' is to discover our reason for being."

I first heard Jim Armstrong more than forty years ago and believe he has been one of the most effective preachers of our time. His fluency and power have been a joy and inspiration to me and to thousands of others. The Roman Quintilian once defined rhetoric as "a good man speaking well." The words that follow reveal a good man thinking and writing well, and in the process, the author has provided a helping hand to all of us.

– George McGovern
U.S. Senator (retired)
1972 Democratic nominee for U.S. President

1

THE DASH BETWEEN

1

You were born. You are alive. You will die. These are irreversible facts—an inescapable life cycle. We have no control over the circumstances related to our births, over the when and the where of our entry into this world. But, what we *do* with the gift of life will determine our earthbound destinies.

My mother is buried in rural Indiana. Over her grave is a simple marker. It reads:

Frances Green Armstrong
1892 – 1976

That's all—but that does not begin to tell the story. The "–" on her gravestone spans the years of her life.

The drama of her years was not unlike that of many of you who read these words. Her father was a lumberman in Minnesota. He was a simple and good man. His wife, a small, wispy Englishwoman, was something of a tyrant. Doubtless unaware of the manner in which her temperament was impacting the lives of her offspring, she imposed her iron will on her son and two daughters. Frances moved through a tense and troubled childhood, daunted by her mother yet dreaming of becoming a teacher. She attended college and after two years received her teacher's certificate. In debt and insecure, she suffered what was then considered a "nervous breakdown." She survived, moved beyond the sad maze of that experience, and became a loving and devoted teacher.

When she was 24 she married a young man who had returned from the Mexican border where he had been sent—as a member of the Montana National Guard—to ward off Pancho Villa and his revolutionaries, or so he was told. My mother was shy and soft-spoken, my father was robust and gregarious, but they loved one another and exchanged their vows. On the original Armistice Day in 1918, a beautiful curly-headed little girl was born to them. She became the center of Frances' life, but tragically, at the age of four, she fell victim to diphtheria and was taken from them. The scars of that loss remained with them across the years that followed.

They moved from Montana to Oregon to Indiana where another daughter was born and then a son—that's me. When I was still a toddler they were involved in an automobile accident and Mother's neck was broken. She survived, but would never again be quite the same.

Her husband became a minister and she became a stereotypical preacher's wife. She taught Sunday school, sang in the choir, played the piano for Wednesday night prayer meetings, and seemed always on hand as a bulwark of strength when her husband's faith wavered and when her youngsters wandered from the straight and narrow. When only 58, my father suffered a fatal stroke. Since her car accident thirty years earlier, Mother had never driven; she learned to drive. After her early stint of teaching she had not been employed; she got a job. With rare grit and determination she lived out her days manifesting a quality of life that inspired and strengthened those around her.

The Frances Armstrong I remember was a marvelous human being. She sat by my bedside when I was a sickly boy, teaching me "numbers" and how to read and write. She never raised her voice in anger, never struck her children. She gave them a remarkable degree of freedom as they grew, enabling them to make their own foolish mistakes. Yet she was always nearby when they stumbled—helping them get back up, brush themselves off and move beyond their misfortune. When I "had to get married" as a teenager, she and my father were there to embrace my youthful bride and to encourage us to cope with whatever the future held for us. I will never know the depths of their disappointment, the tears they doubtless shed, the pain they knew. I only experienced their unconditional, forgiving love.

In her later years Mother was active in her Leisure World community—surrounded by friends, active in her church, listening to and viewing Lawrence Welk and her favorite soaps, and staying in close touch with her children who were now grown with families and careers of their own. At the age of 84 she died of pancreatic cancer.

The circumstances of Frances' life were not unique:

- She had a flawed parent, as many of us have had.
- She dreamed her childhood dreams. Who among us hasn't?
- She left school with a cartload of debts.

- She had a "nervous breakdown." Today we would probably call her illness depression. We too have our inner tempests.
- She married a young man returning home from military service. Many of our parents married after World War II or Korea or Vietnam. Today wars rage in Afghanistan and Iraq, and the veterans, too often terribly scarred, return to our embrace.
- She gave birth to a beautiful child who was taken from her young parents just four years later. Their sense of loss was indescribable.
- A car accident inflicted an injury that became a lifetime source of discomfort.
- She had children, kept house, cooked meals, went to church, raised a family, was active in community affairs. Her children disappointed her. Her husband wasn't always faithful. And when he died at a relatively young age she had to start all over again—learning to drive a car, getting a job, handling her own finances, making new friends, fending for herself, and sometimes feeling terribly alone.

Many circumstances of Frances' life were similar to those of millions of others, like many if not most of us. However, what she did with those circumstances, how she responded to misfortune and loss, the decisions she made and the pathways she chose, determined the substance of the life not detailed by the dash on her gravestone—the blank space, punctuated by a dash, between the years of her birth and death.

The pages that follow will explore the meaning of living and dying with purpose and grace. They will deal with questions we all ask and problems we all face. Who are you, really, and what are you doing here? How can you get out of the boxes you find yourselves in, or are you stuck where you are? What do you believe in, and do your beliefs make any difference? What about the bumps in the road? How can you cope with disappointment, suffering and loss? As you age are you continuing to learn and grow, or are you simply getting old? And, what about death—the loss of loved ones and your own mortality? Are you frightened by the specter of an uncertain, unfathomable future?

My graduate studies were in the field of psychotherapy. I have spent a professional lifetime counseling people. As I have formed the words on these pages, I have drawn on that background and those experiences. I now teach a variety of courses at Rollins College in Florida. One of the staples of my courses is the use of biography. I have my students write short social and psychological sketches of persons who have helped shape the world around them. I will do the same in these pages, developing brief story lines taken from the lives of an assortment of persons—some well-known, some obscure and unknown—who have much to teach us. Some of the lessons will be positive, some negative. But they will be applied to our fears and frustrations, to our hopes and dreams.

Along the way I will explore an assortment of convictions with you:

- You are a unique, free and responsible person.
- You have hidden depths that need to be explored and relied upon.
- You will encounter hardship and suffering.
- You will probably have doubts along the way.
- You can cope with and learn from your suffering; you can move beyond your doubts.
- You can experience your mortality with both purpose and grace.

In all of this I will try to blend matters of social concern and public policy with the private precincts of your soul.

2

PURPOSE AND GRACE

2

One of the keys to our personhood is our ability to choose—in other words, our freedom. The fact is, we are not free not to choose. True, the time, place and circumstances of our birth impose obvious limitations on us. We are not free to be a courtesan in 19th century France or to wage war in ancient Greece. We are not free to be a disciple of Jesus or Siddhartha Gautama (the Buddha) during their lifetimes. We are not free to be a person other than who we are. But, apart from the obvious, each one of us is called upon to exercise a sometimes frightening degree of freedom. In a very real sense, we are the masters of our fates. With that in mind, let's move on to a consideration of the opportunities and challenges that the gift of life brings to each of us.

You are a human being, a unique, one-and-only person. Viktor Frankl, a Viennese psychiatrist and Holocaust survivor, once wrote, "A human being is not one thing among others; *things* determine each other, but *persons* are ultimately self-determining. What we become—within the limits of endowment and environment—we make of ourselves." As a dear old friend of mine used to say, "Every tub's gotta sit on its own bottom."

For each of us, life is a quest. We move from childhood through adolescence and into adulthood—setting goals, making choices, encountering difficulties, stumbling and occasionally falling. But we're moving, always moving, involved in the process of becoming whoever we one day will be. Not one of us is a finished product.

There are momentary flashes of rare insight. Some time ago I was talking with an alcoholic who was being "dried out." She was filled with remorse and seemed determined to regain her self-respect. I suggested she set some goals for herself. What kind of a person did she want to become? What kind of emotional climate did she want to inhabit? Where did she want to be in another ten years? We parted with those questions lingering in her mind.

The following day we met again. She sank into a chair and said, "I didn't sleep last night. Suddenly I realized I had never consciously selected a goal for myself. I've never tried to go anywhere." That was an overstatement. Of course she had set goals for herself. Where would she go to school? Would she study or not study? Would she date? Would she smoke? Drink? Have sex? Would she marry? Where would she live? It goes without saying that she had made day-to-day decisions. However, she was facing the fact that much of her life had been a wasteland. She had drifted aimlessly without consciously setting important goals and developing clearly defined guidelines. "I have never tried to go anywhere." Successful living requires a determination to go somewhere, to embrace a meaningful set of values and objectives. What are the overarching purposes of our lives?

When we are children our aims are simply defined. Normally we seek parental approval. We want our teachers and friends to like us. As we grow older we have to deal with the unforeseen and the unpredictable. We become more self-aware. The landscape of opportunities becomes more cluttered. Our options increase in number and our decisions become more complicated. Sometimes the darkness of adversity descends upon us early in life as it did for Marguerite Johnson.

Marguerite was born black into a cruelly segregated society. Her parents were divorced when she was only three. When she was six her mother's boyfriend raped her. An uncle killed the man. The trauma of that event caused her to be mute for six years.

After being brutalized again she ran away, going to Los Angeles to live in a junkyard with other homeless children. She became pregnant at sixteen and gave birth to a son. Her life in the junkyard changed her. She became aware of the fact that she was a human being—part of a human community.

She wrote:

> *My thinking processes so changed that I hardly recognized myself.*
> *The unquestioning acceptance of my peers had dislodged the familiar*
> *insecurity. After hunting down unbroken bottles and selling them*
> *with a white girl from Missouri, a Mexican girl from Los Angeles and*
> *a black girl from Oklahoma, I was never again to sense myself so*
> *solidly outside the pale of the human race. The lack of criticism*
> *evidenced by our ad hoc community influenced me and set a tone of*
> *tolerance in my life.*[1]

Her self-acceptance and the realization that she was part of a social reality beyond herself were necessary first steps, but the transformation was slow in coming. As a single mother in her early twenties, faced with harsh reality, she danced in a strip joint, was a prostitute, ran a brothel, and was married and divorced. As a performer she sang and danced in San Francisco and toured with Gershwin's *Porgy and Bess* and Jean Genet's *The Blacks*. Marguerite Johnson had adopted a stage name—Maya Angelou.

As a little girl Marguerite had scribbled poems, had been nurtured by the music of the black church, and was introduced to a black school library in her town. At the age of seven she began to read everything she could lay her hands on, "even if (she) didn't understand it."

Years went by and she became a songwriter, a playwright, a film producer and director, and a distinguished author. She was a journalist in the Middle East and editor of the *African Review* in Ghana. A civil rights activist, she was a coordinator for the Southern Christian Leadership Conference. She befriended and worked beside both Malcolm X and Martin Luther King, Jr. In 1968 she was working with Dr. King in Memphis, helping organize the Poor People's March, when he was slain on April 4th—her 40th birthday.

She was awarded a fellowship by Yale University and has been a university professor. But before she became famous and the accolades started coming her way, she was the first black woman to operate a San Francisco trolley car. She emerged from the trials of her early life with an indomitable spirit. From her humble beginnings, driven by an inner fire, Maya Angelou has become one of the most inspirational figures of our time, motivated by the noblest of purposes and exuding a wondrous aura of grace.

In 1970, she wrote *I Know Why the Caged Bird Sings*. In 1983, she wrote another award-winning book, *Shaker, Why Don't You Sing?* Why don't we? If Maya Angelou, with such a damaged childhood, could sing songs of hope and confidence, why can't we?

Think of it. She had been raped and otherwise abused. She had been struck dumb by violence. A runaway, she had found a home among the homeless. Together, in the direst of circumstances, a group of outcast girls created a community. Slowly, Marguerite redefined herself. Moving far beyond the cheap and tawdry—beyond remorse and self-pity, refusing to become a victim of cruel circumstance—she refocused her life on the interests, the needs and the aspirations of others. She became the Maya Angelou the world has come to know and love.

The simple serenity of Maya Angelou's lovely Harlem brownstone home may seem far removed from Tibetan Buddhism, but it isn't. The attainment of *nirvana* in Tibetan Buddhism—a state of "perfect enlightenment"—is said to result from embracing and practicing the eightfold path of right understanding, right thought, right speech, right action, right livelihood, right effort, right mindfulness, and right concentration. These activities and ways of thought lead to the cultivation of wisdom and compassion. A Buddhist representation of compassion is called *chenrezig*.

The Chenrezig Project has been developed in central Florida by Mark Winwood. His story is worth sharing.

A few years ago Winwood was a high-rolling, hard-driving businessman. He was hobnobbing with Manhattan's most successful, commuting between New York and San Francisco, running up $20,000 a month on his corporate credit card—vainly trying to balance an all-consuming career with a marriage and three youngsters. He says, "As you got to know me, you learned that I wasn't balancing things all that well. If you could have seen inside you would have seen this guy who was going to crash one day." And crash he did. His company failed, as did his marriage. He went through a devastating divorce. While trying to recover, he realized how empty his life was, how bitter, stressed and discombobulated he had become. He had lost any sense of meaning or any real connection with the world around him.

As his life was coming apart at the seams his devoted mother died. He was left an inheritance, an amount that bankrolled two pilgrimages to India where he would try to rethink his values and "find himself." He spent time in monasteries with Buddhist monks and nuns. He entered into their exercises and disciplines. He went into the Himalayas, to Dharmsala, the home of the Dalai Lama, and studied the teachings of that remarkable spiritual leader.

From the monks he says he learned the worth of three things: 1) digesting what you learn from discussion, 2) teaching, and 3) meditating. He says, "Those three acts make a difference about what's inside you." One of the exercises he was exposed to required his envisioning his own death and "talking through it." It taught him to say things that seem strangely out of character for a Western male mindset. Reflecting on it at the time, he said: "I tell people that I love them. I never used to do that. It feels really good to say it. It's real. It's right. You become more compassionate and accepting of yourself."

Winwood has become a Tibetan Buddhist teacher. He established his Chenrezig Project that features weekly study groups, the teaching of meditation techniques and ways in which life can be infused with compassion. Winwood, who is in his 50s and looks like a burly, scrappy truck driver, says he is continuing to work on his *intentions* (objectives) that he might move beyond self-centeredness to demonstrate the grace of compassionate other-centeredness.

Maya Angelou and Mark Winwood—two persons who came from radically different backgrounds. Each experienced hardship, as most of us do, and each struggled to regain a reason for being. Each outgrew crippling self-centeredness to achieve aims and purposes beyond the self. And each embraced *charis*—a Greek word meaning "grace" or "loving-kindness"— a compassionate understanding of and relationship to the people among whom they lived.

WHAT DO AN ALCOHOLIC drying out in a rehab center, the incomparable Maya Angelou and a Tibetan monk have to do with you? It is probable that many of you can echo the plaintive cry of the woman who confessed, "I have never tried to go anywhere." You may be trapped in a loveless marriage or in a job that pays little and satisfies less. You may be a university student who doesn't have the slightest idea what you should be preparing for. You may be a mechanic who comes to the end of each workday with grimy clothes, greasy hands, dirty fingernails and an aching back—wondering if this is all life has to offer.

Or, you may be like a very old man I sat with as he was dying. He had been the editor of a Canadian newspaper. Now, far from home on a strange bed, his frail body turned toward the wall as he wept and moaned, "It's all been waste. It's all been waste." And then he slipped away. What a sad ending to what might have been a distinguished career. Age, sex, race and social class have little to do with the absence of purpose or sense of direction. The fact is, each one of us needs to define her or his own meanings and beliefs lest we become wandering nomads.

When the Greek philosopher says, "Know thyself," he may be speaking directly to some of us. Our self-discovery may not be as dramatic as that of Maya Angelou or Mark Winwood, but it can be every bit as significant for us. A psychotherapist can't do it for you. A career counselor can't do it. Preachers and teachers can't do it. Books and articles can't do it. Only *you* can turn your life around. The first step in doing this is to examine your core beliefs.

3

WHAT YOU BELIEVE
IS IMPORTANT

3

Purpose and grace are not easily come by. Living with purpose and grace is not simple. Rick Warren is pastor of one of America's largest mega-churches. As many of you know, he has written *The Purpose Driven Life* (2002), one of the most widely read books of our time—nearly 30 million copies have been sold. It offers readers a 40-day personal spiritual journey outlining what Warren calls God's five purposes for our lives. What are we here for? He says we are all called to worship, fellowship, discipleship, ministry and mission. Without question the book has helped countless people—some dramatically.

In March of 2005, an escaped prisoner who had shot a judge, a court reporter, a sheriff's deputy and a customs official, raged into the Atlanta apartment of Ashley Smith and took her hostage at gunpoint. He bound her in a bathtub. From that hapless position she maintained her poise and talked to him about her own troubled past. A bond seemed to develop between them. He untied her. She showed him pictures of her family and reasoned that if he hurt her, her little girl "wouldn't have a mommy or a daddy." She talked to him about God's power and read to him from Rick Warren's book about service to others. She pled with him to turn himself in, go to prison, and "share the word of God" with other inmates. He left her and turned himself in.

But there's a rub. Warren insists that those who don't "accept Christ" will go to hell. A Jewish reporter once asked him about that, and Warren replied that it wasn't his opinion. That, he argued, is what Jesus said. Warren insists that the Sermon on the Mount is "the greatest sermon ever preached." However, refusing to move beyond his literalistic fundamentalism, he has failed to apply the spirit of that sermon, with its love ethic and emphasis upon personal wholeness and other-centered living, to the larger world around us.

In the same vein as Rick Warren, Cal Thomas, the newspaper columnist who once worked for the Moral Majority, questioned Barack Obama's faith because Obama had once criticized some believers for suggesting that "if people haven't embraced Jesus as their personal savior they're going to hell." But, think for a moment. What about 1.5 billion Muslims? Are they going to hell? What about nearly a billion Hindus, half a billion Buddhists and fifteen million Jews? What about billions of people who dwell in the darkness of poverty, ignorance and oppression, who have never been exposed to God-concepts and religious teachings? What about honest doubters, good agnostics and moral atheists?

Let's personalize the equation. What about the Dalai Lama, Mahatma Gandhi, or the remarkable Nobel laureate Aung San Suu Kyi, who has been kept under house arrest for nearly fifteen of the last twenty years in Myanmar? Their lives of prayer and meditation make the religious practices of most orthodox Christians pale into relative insignificance. I wrote a letter to the editor in response to Cal Thomas' judgmental column saying, "If it's a question of heaven or hell… I would much rather go to hell with Gandhi, the Dalai Lama and Aung San Suu Kyi, than soar off into heavenly 'bliss' with Cal Thomas and his ilk." And I meant it.

The late George Carlin was an acerbic, profane, off-the-wall stand-up comedian. Think of him what you will, some of his observations were disturbingly penetrating. How about this one?

> *Religion has actually convinced some people that there's an invisible man—living in the sky—who watches everything you do, every minute of every day. And the invisible man has a special list of ten things he does not want you to do. And if you do any of these ten things, he has a special place for you, full of fire and smoke and burning and torture and anguish, where he will send you to live and suffer and burn and choke and scream and cry forever and ever 'til the end of time.… But He loves you!*[2]

Don't you see the irony? A god like that would not be worthy of adoration and praise.

Many of you reading these pages reject the exclusive claims and dogmas of sectarianism, yet you genuinely want to move beyond your here-and-now to find a better way. Maybe you believe in God, maybe you don't—and what exactly does that mean? What sort of god do you believe in? Some years ago I read a book on prayer with a chapter titled, "Prayer as dominant desire." The author insisted that the prayers we *really* pray are the overriding interests of our lives. What do we want more than anything else—money, success, many loves, fame; irresponsible pleasure, revenge? Our ambitions (sometimes they become our obsessions) are the prayers we really pray; they are the gods we really serve.

I am convinced that we cannot become what Carl Rogers, one of the 20th century's preeminent psychologists, called "fully-functioning persons"—that is, persons who fulfill much of their individual potential—unless we move beyond self-centeredness to other-centeredness. Now, apply this to yourself. You won't be the person you can become unless and until you outgrow self-worship.

Some years ago a very wise man wrote, "Wealth is not the god of our materialized, greedy society…Wisdom is no god… Social prestige and racism and nationalism are not gods; they are acolytes before the pedestal on which the ego is perched."[3] Don't misunderstand. Your ego is not a bad thing. The pilot is not the enemy of an aircraft—the pilot simply controls the course of a plane's flight. So, too, your ego, as the core of your personhood, is not your enemy. There can be little self-respect—little personal growth—apart from a healthy ego. Your ego will determine the shape of your future; it will define your purposes and intentions. If your goals reflect grasping selfishness, overweening pride in personal appearance and accomplishment, unworthy and self-serving ends—your growth will be stunted and your potential will not be fulfilled. A diseased ego destroys.

THERE ARE MANY WHO INSIST THAT only belief in a personal God can deliver us from moral failure and self-worship. In relating their stories they tell of a particular place or describe a particular process that brought the reality of God into their experience. For them, religion may be an individual thing, bringing them the forgiveness of their sins and the promise of eternal life. Critics of such an individualized quest argue that it simply transfers selfishness to the realm of the spirit. However, there are others who believe that their faith, while offering forgiveness and hope, calls them to compassionate service and personal wholeness as well. In either case, they have known the reassuring warmth of a Presence, both beyond and within themselves.

Others of you, reading these words, find no point of connection. "God" is a word religious people use and, as you have observed religious people, you have little desire to believe what they believe or act the way they do. Too many of the church members you know appear to be a blend of hypocrisy and smug self-righteousness. You have not experienced the God they talk about, nor do you want to.

Sometimes a distorted view of God has had disastrous consequences. You may have heard of Jim Jones, a charismatic Christian minister who founded Peoples Temple in 1956, in Indianapolis. It was an emotional, fundamentalist fellowship with pseudo-socialist teachings. It was an interracial congregation. Most of its members were black. I moved to Indianapolis in 1958 and served a large Methodist church less than a mile north of Peoples Temple. I first met Jones when he was serving as director of the Mayor's Human Rights Commission. He was a pleasant individual who seemed dedicated to interracial harmony and economic justice.

A few years later Jones took his Temple to a town a few miles outside San Francisco. For a brief time he was a major player in California politics, but there was a problem: he was becoming increasingly eccentric and delusional. In 1977, he took 900 of his followers and moved to northern Guyana, where he established a utopian community called Jonestown. By this time Jones claimed that he was a reincarnation of Jesus, Ikhnaton, the Buddha, Father Divine and even Nicolai Lenin. His bizarre practices and rapacious conduct came to the attention of Congressman Leo Ryan. In November, 1978, Ryan, with some staff members, went to Guyana to investigate the charges. Realizing that his lewd behavior, pedophilia, and other unjust excesses were about to be exposed, Jim Jones had his supporters kill Ryan and members of his party. He then led 914 of his followers, including 276 children, to drink cyanide-laced Kool-Aid. It was the largest recorded mass suicide in human history.

Or take David Koresh (birth name, Vernon Howell), another charismatic leader. He became head of a group expelled from the Seventh-day Adventist denomination known as the Branch Davidians. He insisted that the end of the world was at hand, a fulfillment of the biblical prophecy of the Seven Seals, and that he was the Messiah returned to earth. Insisting on his "Christhood," he and his followers gathered a huge cache of armed weapons in a ranch outside of Waco, Texas, preparing for a final showdown.

Served papers by state and federal authorities in February of 1993, Koresh refused to submit to governmental pressure and fired on the law enforcement agents, killing four of them. A fifty-one day siege ensued, with Koresh misleading the authorities and then goading them into assaulting the compound—a fulfillment of biblical prophecy, he said. As a result, FBI agents lobbed canisters of tear gas into the buildings. A fire broke out, and 74 Davidians, including 24 children, were burned to death.

Both Jones and Koresh took the easy way out, shooting themselves instead of enduring the agony of cyanide or fiery flames.

What we believe about God, and our relationship to that God, can make a huge difference in how we function. What we believe is just that important. Our beliefs can lead to personal fulfillment and society's betterment, or they can contribute to individual and societal brokenness and destruction.

A spate of best-selling books attacking religion has been written in recent years by atheist scholars including Richard Dawkins, Christopher Hitchens and Sam Harris. Harris, in *The End of Faith* (2004), argues that religious people have waged savage and unjust wars, condoned torture and violence, countenanced slavery, repressed or prohibited the expression of normal and desirable sexual feelings, and have based their approach to life on myths and fairy-tales. In the next chapter, however, we will learn from the Dalai Lama how religion and spirituality should not be confused with one another. Even Harris agrees. He writes, "Our religious traditions are defunct and politically ruinous," yet goes on to speak of the desirability of bringing "reason, spirituality and ethics together in our thinking about the world." He says we are all linked together. "We want to be happy; the social feeling of love is one of our greatest sources of happiness; and love entails that we be concerned for the happiness of others."

What we believe is important. Do our beliefs force us to look and think beyond ourselves? The world's great religions and committed secular humanists agree that we live in a relational universe. Our highest purposes are to cultivate our inner worlds while helping meet the needs of those about us. This is done as we love others even as we love ourselves. It is done as we experience and reflect grace.

4

YOU ARE A MYSTERY –
YOU ARE SPIRIT

4

If we are to move from crippling self-centeredness to grace and other-centered love, how are we to go about it? We can read all the self-help books and self-improvement tracts available, grit our teeth, and mutter, "I'm going to turn my life around"—but it's not that easy. It's just not something we decide to do, and do it.

"Other-centered love" in the abstract is one thing, but we are not dealing with theories and abstractions. Who is the "other" I am supposed to love? A hopelessly disagreeable fellow worker? A mischief-making youngster who lives next door? A child molester? An elderly uncle who suffers from Alzheimer's and makes impossible demands on my time and energy without even realizing it? A drunken marauder who invades my home? Really! Why do I care why they do what they do? I can't be expected to "love" everyone, can I?

No wonder Dostoevsky's "society woman" cried, "Love in action is a harsh and dreadful thing compared to love in dreams." But wait. Forget the immediate context of your world. Instead, ask yourself what transcendent realities, if any, give meaning to your life. As we have insisted, your belief system is that important.

Here we need to be cautious. Be wary of those who insist they have all the answers. Dogmatic ideologues, whether political or religious, undermine a free and responsible society. Like right-wing talk show hosts and columnists, they can appeal to our irrational, darker sides through the airwaves and with the printed word. Like too many televangelists, they can appeal to our uninformed and angry prejudices. Like al-Qaeda terrorists or anti-abortion zealots, they can bomb their "enemies" as they define them. Any belief system that violates the Golden Rule (treat others as you want to be treated), that contradicts the tenets of other-centered love, undermines the common good. For guidance we need to look within ourselves and well beyond ourselves. These are the hidden depths we need to explore.

Consider two words: Spirit and Mystery. And let's begin by turning our gaze inward. You, yes *you,* are an unfathomable entity. You are flesh and blood, bones and marrow, salt, potassium and water—but the chemical components of your being do not begin to explain *you.* The world's many religions and philosophies have tried to define and explain *you.*

The Hindu believes in the *atman,* the eternal "soul," the true "self" of every person. Taoism believes that *qi* is the essential energy of the universe and that each one of us is a microcosm of the universe, part of its spiritual energy. Buddhism, with its emphasis on meditation, enlightenment and spiritual development, believes that the soul inhabits and gives meaning to the body. Shinto, the native religion of Japan, is seen as "the philosophy of the gods"—that is, "the way of the spirit." Judaism insists that God breathed into man the breath of life and he became a "living soul." Christianity teaches that God is Spirit and that our spirits can commune with that Holy Spirit. The primary mission of the Christian faith, according to many, is the salvation of souls.

We need to understand, however, that not one of these religions or ways of thought encompasses ultimate Truth. Ultimate Truth is incomprehensible. However, each of these approaches to the meaning of life sees the individual as a spirit-motivated and energized being—and sees God, or the gods, as unfathomable, beyond human understanding, as awe-inspiring spiritual reality.

In trying to move away from self-centeredness to other-centeredness we need to look both deep within and well beyond ourselves; we need to discover the benefits and riches of spirituality. One need not be particularly religious in order to be spiritual. In fact, there are those who substitute the rites and forms of religion for honest self-searching and personal growth and are the poorer for it. The by-products of genuine spirituality provide the grace that is requisite for a life well lived. The Christian apostle Paul listed those by-products. He called them "fruits of the spirit." They were love (*agape*), joy, peace, patience, kindness, goodness, faithfulness, gentleness and self-control. These are qualities of life and values that most, if not all, of the world's religions praise. They are qualities that are nurtured within us as we turn away from the altars of self-worship.

Albert Einstein was considered by many to be the greatest scientist of the 20th century. Born in 1879 of Jewish parents, he grew up in Munich, received religious training and was immersed in the lore of the Old and New Testaments and the Talmud. He became deeply religious and fell in love with the music of Mozart and Beethoven. He composed songs "to the glory of God" and learned to play the violin.

He mastered the art of learning. He taught himself calculus, studied advanced engineering, and was fascinated by light. He wondered "what things might look like if someone went along for the ride with a light wave, keeping pace with it as it traveled through space." He developed his theory of relativity, demonstrating the relationship between mass, energy and gravitation. He worked on a unified field theory. (Believe me, I don't begin to understand any of this.) Considered one of the fathers of the atomic age, he was awarded the Nobel Prize for his work in theoretical physics. He was a genius.

What was his belief system? In his youth he began to question both religious and political authority. He left the virulent anti-Semitism of Nazi Germany in 1932 and came to teach at Princeton University. He turned away from Talmudic rules and ways of thought. He described many Bible stories as "pretty childish" and considered Jewish people "no better than other human groups." "I cannot see anything 'chosen' about them," he wrote. Yet, he was neither an atheist nor was he hostile to religion. He came to refer to God as "cosmic intelligence" and was awed by the wonderful harmony and rational beauty of the universe. He once wrote:

> *My religion consists of a humble admiration of the illimitable superior Spirit who reveals himself in the slight details we are able to perceive with our frail and feeble minds. The deeply emotional conviction of the presence of a superior reasoning Power, which is revealed in the incomprehensible universe, forms my idea of God.*[4]

There you have it. Spirit and Mystery.

But what kind of man was Einstein? He was unbelievably humble. He was a renowned humanitarian. He was a lifelong pacifist who was opposed to war and who cried out against the use of the atomic bomb. He was dedicated to some form of world government. Having experienced Hitler's Germany he worked tirelessly to help loved ones and strangers alike flee fascism in Europe. He once wrote Israel's Prime Minister David Ben-Gurion saying, "…my relationship to the Jewish people has become my strongest human bond, ever since I became fully aware of our precarious situations among the nations of the world." In 1952, he was offered the presidency of the State of Israel. Honored and deeply moved as he was, he wrote that he was "both saddened and ashamed that [he] could not accept it."

Although he occupied a unique place on the world stage, Einstein lived a life of selfless simplicity. He found enjoyment in sailing and music. He shuffled around the Princeton campus wearing baggy clothes, puffing on his pipe, refusing to wear socks, absorbed in his scientific thought world. His daughter, Margot, and his sister, Maja, shared his household on the Princeton campus. His sister suffered a severe stroke and was bedridden. Month after month, night after night, he read to her until she died in 1951. His gentle spirit and concern for others gave special meaning to his scientific endeavors.

Most of us want to be happy. We want to enjoy life and avoid heartaches and personal problems. Sigmund Freud, the father of psychoanalysis, said that we reveal what our purposes and intentions in life are by our behavior. He wrote, "We want to be happy and remain so." He went on to confess, and most of us would agree, that "unhappiness is much less difficult to experience." How true. Many of us may be unhappy because our understanding of happiness is shallow and self-serving. The Dalai Lama, one of the most revered world leaders of our time, appears to consider the achievement of happiness a primary goal in life. He lectures about it and writes best-selling books about it. But to him, happiness is a byproduct of spirituality. He writes, "Spirituality I take to be concerned with those qualities of the human spirit—such as love and compassion, patience, tolerance, forgiveness, contentment, a sense of responsibility, a sense of harmony—which bring happiness to both self and others." Freud believed that happiness is fleeting because it is based on physical pleasure. The Dalai Lama insists that "the unifying characteristic of the qualities I have described as 'spiritual' may be said to be some level of concern for others' well-being... To speak of spirituality in any terms other than these is meaningless." Your happiness and mine are rooted in other-centered spirituality.

Some translations of the Beatitudes in Jesus' Sermon on the Mount substitute the word "happy" for "blessed."

Happy are those who sense their spiritual need—for the heavenly realm is theirs.
Happy are the sorrowful—for they will be consoled.
Happy are the humble—for they will possess the land.
Happy are those who yearn for right living—for they will be satisfied.
Happy are the merciful—for they will be shown mercy.
Happy are the pure in heart—for they will see God.
Happy are the peacemakers—for they are the children of God.

Happy are you if you are persecuted in the cause of right—that's the way it's always been with prophetic voices.

– **Matthew 5:3-11 (paraphrased)**

Some of these "promises" are hard to believe; take, for instance, that bit about inheriting the earth and ultimately prevailing. But, whatever else these teachings signify, they mean that—as in the mind of Jesus, the thought of the Dalai Lama and the daily walk of Albert Einstein—humility, compassion and other-centered "singleness of purpose" (another translation of "purity of heart") are interconnected and bound together with a deeper understanding of happiness and spirituality.

So once again, how do we move from living self-centered to other-centered lives? We plumb the depths. We are summoned to a contemplative life style. Granted, we are not nuns or monks, not priestesses or rabbis, probably not even overtly religious. Here we turn to the Dalai Lama once again. He writes: "… I have come to the conclusion that whether or not a person is a religious believer does not matter much. Far more important is that they be a good human being."[5]

And meditation, contemplation and prayer are pathways to becoming a "good human being."

5

MEDITATION, CONTEMPLATION AND PRAYER

5

I won't suggest spiritual exercises for you that I do not practice myself, so let me do a bit of soul-baring. My wife Sheri and I get up each morning at about 6:30. We sit in our breakfast nook, chat, sip our coffee and read the newspapers—our local Sentinel and the New York Times. I try to complete the crosswords, scrub the printers ink off my hands, kiss Sheri farewell for the morning, and head upstairs to my study/office. My students call it my "Zen hideaway."

I have a book on Eastern religions in which each chapter, devoted to one of the world's religions, has a section entitled "Sacred Time" and one called "Sacred Space." The specific "sacred times" I have carved out for my daily meditations are early mornings and late evenings. The specific "sacred spaces" are my study and my bedroom.

My devotional life consists of three basic ingredients: remembrance, gratitude and intentions. So that you will better understand the "Zen hideaway" reference, let me describe my study. It contains bookshelves, a wraparound computer desk, a table I use as a more formal desk (for study, writing and stuff like that) and file cabinets. There are photographs, paintings and mementoes on walls, desktops, shelves—everywhere. Let me tell you about some of them.

Above my computer on one wall are five photos: one of "Jimmy Mac," my godson and namesake, who died of AIDS at the age of 25; one of Ben Garrison, a lifelong friend and colleague; one of Mike McIntyre, a young co-worker who labored by my side in the trenches of political and ecclesiastical conflict; one of Jim Allison and me (Jim was "Big Jim," a huge African American academician and activist, who was a nagging presence in corridors of power as we tried to bring black and white segments of our town together); and one of Jim Grant, a friend for half a century, who struggled for years with dementia and diabetes and slipped away in 2010. (When one is my age remembrance is sometimes a sad and poignant thing.)

On the desk to my left is a collage of photographs taken long years ago of four generations of Armstrongs: one of my grandfather, my father, my infant son, and myself; one of my parents with my sister and me in our teens; assorted shots of our small children; and one of me as an eighteen-year-old in my Navy uniform. There are more recent shots of my "children" (no longer children) and of my beloved Sheri. And there is one of Senator Ted Kennedy and one of me and my Iliff School of Theology faculty colleagues.

The walls hold a Diego Rivera print, an El Greco print, a Mayan tile calendar, an icon given me by the Patriarch of the Russian Orthodox Church, a colored etching of the magnificent Spanish Byzantine chapel at Rollins College where I have taught for nearly twenty years, and a calligraphy created for me by Kim Dae-Jung when he was under house arrest in Seoul. Kim would later be elected President of South Korea, and would receive the Nobel Peace Prize in 2000. The calligraphy—an adage surviving the Sino-Japanese war—reads, "To Serve Man Is to Serve Heaven." There is also a prized photo of George McGovern, with the inscription, "For Jim…a treasured friend."

So, each morning as I begin my meditation, my eyes scan the walls, search the bookshelves, single out particular mementoes, and I remember and thank whatever gods may be. My life has known its share of pain and suffering, as has each one of yours, but, oh, how rich and full it has been! Frankly, most of my prayers are "thank yous," expressions of gratitude for friends and family, for myriad opportunities and a vast array of experiences.

Normally, during this time of early morning reflection, I think of the particular needs of those who come to mind (can I respond in any way?): of the Rollins students I must prepare for, of the conversations I must have, the letters I must write and the people I must see. I focus on my aims and intentions. I ask for guidance and wisdom. What I do sounds suspiciously like prayer—and of course it is. Yet, I have no firm convictions about prayer. Is God a personal god who "hears" and "responds"? Frankly, I don't know. I do not believe in a bellhop god—a god who suspends the laws of nature while responding to my every selfish whim. I don't believe in a divine magician in a far-off sky. It may be that prayer is self-delusion as the gods respond with a sobering silence. But if, as I believe, there is a "divine intelligence," and if spirit can commune with Spirit, then the mystery of self-transcendence prevails. In any event, acts of meditation and reflection enrich my soul and, I hope, enrich the lives of others.

Another sacred time is bedtime, after the lights are out and the tasks of the day are behind me. That is roll call time: I pray for my first family, one by one, as I know of their particular needs; my second family, one by one; next, my third family (like many of you, I have been married more than once) and then come friends and acquaintances in crisis or with special needs. Is there anything I can do to demonstrate my helpful concern? Empathy, compassion and determined response are at the heart of this form of reflection.

There is yet another sacred time. It can be *any* time—as you do the dishes or drive your car while running errands or as you loll by the pool, basking in the brilliance of Florida sunshine, or stretch out before a fireplace in the Pacific Northwest (where you live does make a difference). Years ago I came upon a little novel by Bruce Marshall called *The World, the Flesh and Father Smith* (1945). It told of an elderly priest who, as he went about the tasks of his day, would spot passers by—washerwomen, workmen, playing children, clerks and truck drivers—and, as he saw them, he would mutter brief intercessory prayers. Not a bad habit. At least it transfers our mental activities from self-absorption to the realities of other lives.

Does this recital of my contemplative habits suggest that you should "go thou and do likewise"? Of course not. Do your own thing. But, do it!

Let's assume that you are just beginning this inner journey. Actually, it makes little difference whether you are just beginning or are well on your way. Contemplation, meditation, prayer—call your practice what you will—requires *silence*. Noises are distracting. Relax. Let your muscles and your thinking processes quiet down. Eastern religions, with their emphases upon stillness and enlightenment, have much to teach us. Mystics speak of "practicing the Presence." That requires receptivity—the ability to listen. In our quiet time, we need the ability to respond to the impulses and whisperings of a transcendent Spirit.

Life in the spirit is not passive—it is active. It requires our participation. I have already suggested that reading self-help books and self-improvement tracts won't remold our inner worlds. But inspirational materials and the writings of the mystics can provide guidelines. The sacred writings of Buddhism, with their emphasis on the essential oneness of the universe and everything in it, and the enrichment or "liberation" of personality with a corresponding loss of anxiety and fear, are profoundly meaningful. Quakers like Rufus Jones and Elton Trueblood, and other Christian mystics like Thomas Merton, Henry Nouwen, St. Teresa, Evelyn Underhill, Kenneth Leech and Anthony Bloom, can inspire us.

Sometimes we accidentally stumble into the presence of transformational material. Long years ago when I was a college student preparing for my professional career, I rummaged through a used bookstore and came upon a rare bargain—five volumes of sermons crammed into an 840-page book that was on sale for $1.50. The author was a young 19th-century English clergyman named Frederick W. Robertson. I didn't know him from Adam, but I knew a bargain when I saw one, so I purchased it. It became the basis of my devotional life for many months. His critical evaluation of institutional religion, his fierce identification with the least among us, and his unusual insight as he wrote about doubt, loneliness, suffering and forgiveness, spoke to some of my internal struggles at the time. Do your own digging. Ask for recommendations from friends and counselors. Browse through bookstores. Let your reading become a rewarding adventure.

There is nature. The natural wonders of our country are almost beyond belief. Many of us live within a stone's throw of awesome mountain ranges, gentle streams, rugged coastlines, desert wilderness or forest glades. Those less fortunate may be surrounded by the bleak and the barren. But wherever we live and whoever we are, we can see starry skies at night, and most can view the wonders of sunrises and sunsets. We may live in densely populated cities or sprawling suburban neighborhoods. But in spite of the ugliness of so much urban life and the sameness of so much suburban dwelling, we can concentrate on the throbbing humanity and promising vitality around us. We can be selective in the things we choose to see and feel. Many evenings my wife and I sit in the space behind our home, look through the foliage above us, discuss the events of the day or maintain our silences—and all the while feel a sense of reverence for the gift of life. Whatever your settings or whoever your companions, determine to gratefully concentrate on the beauty that is available to you. It is there. Embrace it and revel in it.

There is music and the arts. We don't have to go to concerts or trudge through museums in order to be entertained. Most of us have radios or television sets. We can select what we listen to and view. Our home, though small, is a miniature art gallery. Our oldest son is an accomplished painter, and we have some of his works on our walls. We have three Monets and a Van Gogh (not even close to originals, they are framed prints purchased for a few dollars), and a small version of "The Thinker" by Rodin. We can create our own oases of beauty in our immediate surroundings.

We have been exploring our inner worlds, considering contemplative life styles. The ability to relax and go with the flow, to use our imaginations and discipline ourselves, are parts of the journey. Seasons of silence, inspirational literature, the wonders of nature, music and the arts—all have their contributions to make. Let scientists and astronomers probe the vastness of outer space. We have our own inner space to deal with.

6

ABOUT VALUES
AND "THE GOOD"

6

"We hold these truths to be self-evident, that all men are created equal, that they are endowed by their Creator with certain unalienable Rights, that among these are Life, Liberty and the pursuit of Happiness." If you are like most U.S. citizens, you were made to memorize those words from the United States Declaration of Independence when you were a youngster. An earlier draft made reference to "Property," but our founding fathers came to realize that material goods cannot guarantee a good life, nor is their possession an inherent right. Rather, they said that the pursuit of happiness *is* a human right.

The pursuit of happiness is a two-edged sword. It can be as self-absorbed and self-serving as pagan sin. Or, as the Dalai Lama, the Nazarene carpenter, and sages of every faith and age have suggested, it can be a byproduct of spirituality. They have said we are happy as we cultivate qualities of inner strength and other-centered compassion.

To some degree we have already thought about life, liberty and happiness. They are values representing "the good."

We began with individual worth. Life, personal life, your life, is an inestimable gift. A European philosopher named Emil Brunner once wrote that values exist "only in reference to persons." Some of us reading these pages consider ourselves pro-life; others of us are pro-choice. Perhaps most of us consider ourselves both. We believe in the unique worth of the person, and we believe that a woman has the right to control her own body. We don't understand the ancient debates of the Church Fathers about the "ensoulment" of the fetus. When does an embryo become a person? When does life begin? Who can pretend to speak with ultimate authority on that one? But most of us do believe personal life is unique. It is a gift we claim and a personal right that gives meaning to all others. However, we don't always treat people as if they are special, nor has everyone always treated us as if we were special.

I remember a first-grade teacher who yanked me out of my seat and shook me (I probably deserved it). I remember standing in our kitchen and slapping my teenage daughter (I have been haunted by that memory for more than fifty years, hoping and praying that she has long since forgotten it—and doubting she has). Think of the people you know: the wife who has been betrayed and humiliated by her husband's infidelity; the businessman who has been fleeced by a trusted partner he regarded as a friend; the youngster who is blamed for a costly prank he had nothing to do with; the elderly parent who, against her will, has been stashed away in a seedy nursing home; the homosexual who is blamed and shamed by his parents for being who he was born to be. You can take a moment and develop your own list of victims and offenders.

TO BE UNWANTED, ignored or unloved can be a tragic fate. Our culture has trivialized and cheapened "love." But to believe that love—mature, other-centered love—is the reality that binds all good things together is to embrace the essence of creation. It was the ethicist Joseph Fletcher who wrote, "Only one thing is intrinsically good; namely, love: nothing else at all." Love is not simply something we offer, something we give to another. With the passage of time, if we are growing in the right direction, it infuses all of our actions; it defines who we are. To love, unselfishly—in the relationships of home and family; in the demanding responsibilities of industry and commerce; in the give-and-take of social action and statecraft, promoting "the general welfare"—is to discover our reason for being.

Life, *liberty,* and the pursuit of happiness—our founders were thinking of "taxation without representation" and freedom from the British crown when they penned those words. Our Civil War freed the slaves. World War I was fought, according to President Wilson, to "save the world for democracy." World War II was waged to destroy the totalitarian tyranny of the Axis Powers, the madness of the Holocaust and the enslavement of much of the world. In our own time and in our own country critical questions have been raised about our freedoms: the suspension of habeus corpus, wiretapping and the invasion of privacy, waterboarding and other forms of torture, Guantanamo, Abu Ghraib, and the legitimacy of a preemptive war based on lies and misinformation. What happens in the public square is related to both our national ideals and our most personal worlds.

We have already talked about the indivisibility of spirituality and happiness, and about individual liberty. We are not free not to choose. There is no such thing as un-freedom. The choices we make will determine the course of our lives. Years ago, in the state of North Dakota, a dirt road intersected an interstate highway. As you drove west on the interstate and then turned north on the dirt road you were greeted by a sign that read, "Choose your ruts carefully. You will be in them for the next thirty miles." That's how it is with the choices we make. Some of them may be trivial and inconsequential. But, others can be far more binding, lasting for long years or a lifetime.

LEE TAI-YOUNG WAS ONE of the most remarkable and impressive human beings I have known. Her life featured a series of groundbreaking, courageous decisions. The history of Korea stretches back some 5000 years. She became the first woman attorney in that storied land, and in 1956, she founded a legal aid society for women. Women in South Korea were denied their basic rights: they could not own property; if divorced they could not keep their children; they were not respected, and often brutalized by their husbands. They were emotionally crushed and broken. Moved by their plight, Lee Tai-Young opened an office in downtown Seoul. Sought out by needful women and seeking them out, she moved from her dingy starting place to a more respectable setting.

In 1960, she agreed to serve as dean of the Law School at Ewha University (bear in mind, there were no women lawyers in Korea). For eight years she served in that capacity while continuing her work in what had come to be known as the Legal Aid Center for Family Relations. Above the door of the center a sign read: "Legal Aid Center – the poor and the ignorant receive aid without fee." That policy would never change.

Believing that her center needed a permanent headquarters, she raised $200,000, and purchased a plot of land on Yoido Island—a site where federal buildings stood, ROK troops were reviewed, and where Billy Graham was to speak to more than a million people during one of his crusades.

Her husband, a public servant for three decades, served as foreign minister in the early 1960s. In 1976, he was a member of the National Assembly representing the opposition party. On March 1 of that year, marking the fifty-seventh anniversary of Korea's freedom from Japan's absolute domination, Dr. Lee and her husband signed a human rights petition protesting South Korea's oppressive Yushin Constitution. They were both arrested.

At the time, her building on Yoido Island was under construction. Her trial dragged on for nine months. Not once did she say, "I am guilty," or "I am innocent." She only asked that the judge let her remain free until the building was finished. She was convicted and sentenced to three years in prison—once the six-story building was completed.

Because of the notoriety of the case, the international community protested and her sentence was suspended. But she was disbarred and would not be permitted to vote, serve on boards, occupy any public position, or re-enter her building on Yoido Island.

Physically exhausted and emotionally drained she struggled through two months of depression, and then decided on a course of action. She took small trees and plants from her own yard, crossed the bridge to the island, and planted them on the center grounds. When the scrubwoman for the center quit her job, Lee slipped into the building to become the scrub woman. On all fours she lovingly scrubbed the floors and walls day after day.

The women who worked in the center revered Lee Tai-Young and insisted that she resume her leadership role. If she was arrested they would stand with her and be arrested too. The government probably felt that she would do less harm there than elsewhere and allowed her return to her duties.

She once told me, "All of this has been a gift from God. I was involved in too many things—trying to do too much. Now, God has permitted me to concentrate on the one thing I consider most important. I can give the rest of my life to the women of Korea." That is exactly what she did until her death in 1998.

Think of the decisions she made:

- to become the first female attorney in a male-dominated society;
- to seek justice and human rights for the battered women of her country, an unheard of venture when she first began;
- to become dean of a law school at a women's university when there were no women attorneys in the country (today there are about 50 women in the National Assembly of South Korea and nearly half of them are Ewha graduates);
- to join her husband in protesting the Yushin Constitution;
- to go to prison rather than renounce her ideals, and
- to serve "the poor and ignorant" women of her country as long as she lived.

At the outset of our journey I wrote that we are meant to move beyond crippling self-centeredness to grace and other-centered love. That was true with Lee Tai-Young's journey. She came to live almost exclusively for the sake of others.

The everyday decisions we make may seem like small potatoes when compared to hers: what to put on a grocery list; whether to work overtime or not; whether to watch TV, do the dishes, or mow the lawn; where to go for a vacation. Maybe our goals have been too mundane and self-serving. Remember, our goals should reflect our values. They should express our understanding of "the good." If they haven't been bold enough, daring enough, sufficiently unselfish—it's not too late. The sum total of our decisions, large and small, will determine the content of our lives. "Choose your ruts carefully." Not only that, but don't be content to settle for self-imposed limitations.

7

OUTGROWING
OUR BOXES

7

In our introductory chapter I mentioned the boxes in which we often find ourselves. We feel hemmed in by fate and circumstance—we feel trapped. Harry Houdini was noted as the most accomplished magician of his time. He was an "escapologist." He mastered the art of freeing himself from handcuffs, ropes, vaults, chains, straitjackets, jail cells—restraints of every sort. A psychoanalyst named Adam Phillips wrote a book about him, *Houdini's Box: On the Art of Escape* (2001). Whereas most of Houdini's traps were physical, ours tend to be circumstantial. We find ourselves living in places we don't like, going to jobs that don't satisfy, developing habits we aren't proud of, interacting with people who don't seem to meet our needs, and troubled by negative moods and depression. Too many of us face each new day with a resigned shrug. The drab "same-old-same-old" of every day is getting us down. We feel boxed in, unable to move beyond the here and now.

But we can move. We can grow. In fact, our lives are in constant flux and always changing, consciously or unconsciously, moving in this direction or that. Some forms of growth are inescapable. As children we outgrow toys and clothes and sometimes friends. Our bodies change. I remember the pride I felt when I discovered my first pubic hair, and when I first shaved the peach fuzz from my face. I remember the curiosity I felt when I saw my older sister's Tampax wrapper. Puberty and "the terrible teens" are often times of exciting, confusing and painful change.

Some change is inevitable. Some is intentional. Our intentions and purposes are intertwined. As youngsters our intentions are often vague. We simply function from day to day. We go outside to play. We run errands and do our assigned chores (or make excuses for not doing them). We go to school or ditch school. We try out for a team. If asked out for a date we say "yes" or "no." As we mature, our decisions are more deliberate and complicated. What jobs will we apply for? What college will we attend? What will our major be? Will we go in debt or try to remain debt-free? Our aims and choices determine the direction our lives take.

When Fred Rogers died in 2003, Gloria Steinem, the outspoken feminist and political activist, said that he was "the only person on TV to whom you would trust the future of the world." Fred Rogers—that meek, low-key, self-effacing friend of little children everywhere? Why would Ms. Steinem be impressed with Mr. Rogers? When you were very young did you watch "Mr. Rogers' Neighborhood" on PBS? Did you sit with your children as they watched it? Millions of us across the country did. Maybe, as we watched Rogers' blend of make-believe and value-laden philosophy reduced to concepts and language that the youngest among us could understand, we were being introduced to a pattern of living that could, in fact, serve as a model for our planet's future.

Fred Rogers began his television career in Pittsburgh in 1954, working with children and puppets. From 1968 to 2001, he taped 1,700 "neighborhood" shows, winning every major television award, from the Emmy to the Peabody. He was inducted into the Broadcasting Hall of Fame, gained a star on Hollywood's Walk of Fame, and received our nation's highest civilian award, the Presidential Medal of Freedom.

A gentle, modest man, Fred Rogers was a brilliant, highly trained musician and authority on child development. He wrote some 200 songs, including the jingle he opened every program with:

> *It's a beautiful day in this neighborhood,*
> *A beautiful day for a neighbor.*
> *Would you be mine?*
> *Could you be mine?*

That single ditty may not prove his musical genius, but it asked a fundamental question.

He graduated *magna cum laude* from Rollins College in Florida and attended Pittsburgh Theological Seminary for eight years, limiting himself to one class a term, taken during his lunch break from his television duties. When he graduated he was ordained into the Presbyterian ministry with a charge to continue his work with children.

Fred and Joanne Rogers were both graduates of Rollins. I teach at Rollins. For eight years I served as minister of the Congregational church in Winter Park. Every January when the Rogerses returned to Winter Park to visit family members and enjoy some richly deserved R&R, they attended our church (she sang in the choir). We became good friends. They visited us in our home and we would grab an occasional lunch at Bakely's, his "club"—a poor man's eatery. We corresponded. We talked by phone during his final illness. Believe me—he was exactly the same person in his private life that the world saw in his cardigan sweaters and sneakers on TV.

He once wrote, "At the heart of the universe is a loving heart that continues to beat and that wants the best for every person. Anything we can do to help foster the intellect and spirit and emotional growth of our fellow human beings—that is our job. Those of us who have that particular vision must continue against all odds. Life is for service."[6] Grace and dedication are at the very core of those words.

WE HAVE BEEN THINKING about purpose. As a young man moving into an other-centered career, Rogers listed the qualities of life he wanted to encourage in others. They were self-esteem, self-control, imagination, creativity, curiosity, an appreciation of diversity, cooperation and perseverance. A refrain he repeated over and over again to individual children was, "You are a very special person and I like you exactly as you are." As he conversed with children across the thirty-five years of his public service ministry, he proved that good values can be taught through the mass media.

Obviously, we can't all be Fred Rogers. We may not even want to be pacifist, vegetarian, non-smoking teatotalers. But how much we can learn from the man! From an early age he moved beyond himself and saw life as service to loved ones and strangers alike (although no one was ever a stranger to him). Thousands if not millions of people have been enriched by his life.

Now, think about where you are. Is it where you want to be? Can you recognize desirable areas for self-improvement? What are they? Thinking like Fred Rogers, what traits might you encourage in others?

I grew up in the Midwest. The towns were white, Republican, Protestant, in-grown farming communities—insulated from the world beyond their bounds. *Friends to Make* and *Trips to Take* were two children's books I was made to read in the first and second grades of the elementary school I attended. During those early years my friends were limited to schoolmates, and my trips determined by my parents were usually to the county seat fifteen miles away, or downstate to visit my grandparents in another near-white, conservative town. At least they had a black barber in their 'burg, but I seldom, if ever, saw him.

That's how it is with many of us. Our friends are usually drawn from a small circle of look-alike, think-alike acquaintances. Our trips are usually planned to ease our tensions and reinforce our self-assuring world-views.

We usually vacation in places where we speak the language and our kind of people are relaxing and sightseeing. We don't want our worlds to be disturbed by things different and challenging. It's easier to remain in our boxes, so that's where we stay. But here we are talking about change and growth, about intentional self-cultivation. It may well involve the friends we make and the trips we take.

I remember the first African American people I sought out. One was Ellis, a cook at the YMCA camp where my father was a chaplain. The other was Vivian Postell, a black singer with a magnificent soprano voice, who was brought in to help break down the color barrier at a youth camp where, as a very young minister, I was speaking.

Ellis was a tall, lean black man of indeterminate age. I was a boy eight or nine years old. We would sit on the back steps of the camp kitchen and talk about things I had never heard of and people I had never seen. In my conversations with Ellis, the "darkies" my mother used to talk about were no longer remote images seen in violent wire-photos in newspapers or in exotic articles about Africa in the *National Geographic.* They were flesh and blood human beings who dreamed and laughed and cried like the rest of us.

Vivian Postell grew up in the segregated South in a frame house on a dirt road in Lakeland, Florida. One day we sat under a tree on the shore of Lake Griffith at the youth camp and she shared what it was like for her growing up in Lakeland. She told of a white-robed mob of drunken men lurching down the dirt street in front of her house. Carrying a cross (of all things), they shook their fists and hurled their profane invectives at her family huddled together on their front porch.

She told of her little brother who came running home to tearfully bury his head in her skirts as he described the taunts of a bunch of white youngsters who doubtless had been taught their cruelty by older heads. They had targeted him and shouted, "Nigger! Nigger! Nigger!" Calmly and sadly she spoke of her growing up years, describing things I had no knowledge of nor even imagined.

Almost twenty years ago I returned to Florida and renewed my friendship with Vivian. She had become a distinguished black educator, honored by the state of Florida. She was district lay leader of the church she had been unable to join forty years earlier because of the color of her skin. A street in Lakeland is named for her. She died of cancer not long ago, and her College Heights Church was filled to overflowing with color-blind mourners who grieved her passing. I will be forever in her debt.

In response to the frenzy that was prompted by presidential candidate

Barack Obama's relationship to his pastor, Jeremiah Wright, Obama gave a stirring speech on race in Philadelphia during the 2008 presidential campaign. It was a brilliant, sensitive, historically based analysis of American attitudes and opportunities. I have my students view and analyze it. I commend it to you without reservation.

If racial justice became my cause in the early years of my professional career, equal rights for the GLBT (gay/lesbian/bisexual/transgender) community has become a latter day cause. I have read the books and studied the research. I am absolutely convinced that one's sexuality is a birthright over which he or she has no control. As one of my clients once said, "God don't make mistakes."

As I described my devotional life in the previous chapter, I spoke of five photographs hanging above my computer. Three of the five men were gay. One, my namesake and godson, died of AIDS when he was only 25. The other two were valued colleagues who became close friends. They were brilliant, talented men, with university and graduate degrees, who worked by my side for long months before I learned of their sexuality. They, along with a bishop of the United Methodist Church who turned to me and became a confidante, humanized the issue for me. When we humanize an issue it tends to take on a radically different tone and meaning for us.

THE CRAMPED LIMITATIONS of racial and sexual identity are two of the boxes I think I have outgrown. There have been others. What about you? What prejudices and misconception do you entertain? Have you traced their origins in your life? Are there persons you need to seek out who can help you outgrow the boxes that entrap you? So very much depends on the friends we make and the trips we take. Goshen, Indiana, the county seat fifteen miles from my hometown, where we went for our Christmas shopping (I was given fifty cents to cover all the bases) and a rare movie, seems far removed from Seoul, Harare, Sydney, Moscow and Havana. As professional responsibilities took me to those cities and other radically different locales, the boundaries of my mind were expanded.

In São Paulo, Belo Horizante and Ciudad Juárez I saw the indescribable poverty of barrio/favela (slum) life. In Australia I visited aborigine reserves. In Buenos Aires, Libertad (Uruguay), and Seoul I met with political prisoners. In Havana a small group of us met with Fidel Castro, but we were not permitted to visit prisoners of conscience in his Cuba (nor would the U.S. State Department let us visit Guantanamo). In Harare (then Salisbury) I delivered a United Nations award to Bishop Abel Muzorewa, who had not been permitted to leave Zimbabwe by the Ian Smith government to receive it. In Moscow I met with the patriarch of the Russian Orthodox Church. I also met with Pentecostalists in hiding who were trying to leave the country. During and after the Vietnam War, I joined with a small group of others to talk with U.S. and Vietnamese diplomats, "Third Force" leaders, and political prisoners in Saigon and on Con Son Island. Later I went to Hanoi on a humanitarian aid mission.

You've heard the phrase "mind-blowing"? Well, the experiences these and other travels provided "blew my mind" far beyond the tiny boxes fashioned by my Hoosier boyhood. How could anyone—*anyone*—see and smell the stink of poverty and the vile nature of oppression in Third World countries and remain unmoved? How could anyone—*anyone*—visit lands wasted by senseless wars and see the fruits of defoliation, search-and-destroy missions, shrapnel-shattered little victims suffering in hospitals, sit in on press conferences as military spokesmen and politicians lied, and not be appalled? How could anyone hear the evening news, read the morning paper, or assess arrogant, bullying foreign policies, without harboring reservations and wondering what can be done by people like us? How can anyone go to Darfur, or Somalia, or Baghdad and remain indifferent to the plight of their starving, war-ravaged inhabitants?

In traveling far and wide I realize how singularly fortunate I have been. However, the friends we make and the trips we take don't have to be far-flung and widespread. Youngsters going to local synagogues and mosques to see how other people worship will stretch the borders of their minds. Likewise for underprivileged inner-city children being taken to zoos and museums by concerned neighbors, students going to Mexico or Puerto Rico to refurbish homes for the poor, or going to New Orleans to help clean up after Hurricane Katrina. Miracles of growth take place.

We have been thinking about purpose and grace. It is obvious that, in a world like ours, the selflessness of people like Maya Angelou, Albert Einstein, Gandhi and Mandela, Aung San Suu Kyi, Lee Tai-Young and Fred Rogers stand as beacon lights of hope. But it is not only up to honored leaders and beatified saints—it's up to people like you and me to pave a sane and more promising way. Don't permit the boxes that confine you entrap you. We need to cultivate those relationships and expose ourselves to those realities that will free us from unworthy selfishness and enable us to become the persons we were meant to be.

Is it possible to apply all of this to your present circumstances? How does other-centeredness relate to your here-and-now reality? Do you share your life with a spouse? With your children or parents? What about your work place, your on-the-job relationships? And what about your community activities and ties to church, P.T.A., politics, civic clubs, and labor unions? What values and attitudes are we passing on to others?

A chapter in a book published many years ago was titled, "The Contagion of Who You Are." Remember what Fred Rogers said about fostering growth in the lives of others? Life consists of the tedium of every day. Infuse the routine tasks and intimate relationships of every day with a glad spirit of positive acceptance and an unselfish response to the emotional and physical needs of the people around you. You are a contagious presence in your world. Don't ever tilt toward becoming a contagious disease.

8

SUFFERING —
AND BEYOND

8

Although punctuated by many forms of suffering, few things cause more anguish in our lives than the madness of war. Ask those who have loved ones fighting in the mountains of Afghanistan, or those who have been wounded by roadside bombs in Iraq, or the forgotten men and women in Walter Reed Army Medical Center. Ask those who have lost family members or friends in war.

In spite of the futile insanity of war, we often hear stories of remarkable heroism. Who, by now, hasn't heard of the heroics of John McCain when shot down over Hanoi in 1967? With both arms and a leg broken and a shattered shoulder, he endured 5½ years of solitary confinement and cruel torture in Hoa Lo Prison (the so-called Hanoi Hilton). Today, forty years later, he can't lift his arms high enough to comb his hair. When told of his plight Tammy Duckworth wryly smiles and says, "He can't lift his arms above his shoulders. I can hold my legs above my head." She was a helicopter pilot whose Black Hawk was shot down over Iraq by a rocket-propelled grenade. She had both legs blown off and her right arm shattered in three places. Now she bravely limps on two detachable metal legs.

During the political conventions of 2008, McCain was his party's presidential nominee and we heard his story detailed countless times. Duckworth addressed her party's convention in Denver. McCain is a retired Navy captain and United States Senator, and Duckworth is now second in command for the U.S. Department of Veterans' Affairs. On the issues, they haven't agreed on much of anything. But, think of the *purpose*—the love of country—that drove them to risk and sacrifice. Why we suffer may define our personhood more eloquently than the fact that we have suffered.

Or, we may have no control over our fates. Look at war again. Armed conflict claimed more lives in the 20th century than in all previous centuries of human history combined.

Leningrad, Russia, during World War II, symbolizes the carnage of war.

During the 900-day siege of Leningrad its citizens refused to surrender. Without water and electricity more than half a million of them starved or were frozen to death, yet the besieged people of the city withstood the Nazi hordes on their doorstep.

Many years ago I walked late one night through the vast expanses of the Piskariovskoye Memorial Cemetery in Leningrad. More than 500,000 persons are buried there in 186 mass graves. Never have I been more moved. The somber strains of the 7th Symphony of Shostakovich (the composer's tribute to the victims of the siege) drifted through the night air. The massive monument, dominated by a statue of Mother Russia in the form of a grieving mother with outstretched arms, looked down upon us. Unashamedly, I wept. That memorial cemetery bears eloquent tribute to the hundreds of thousands of people who were willing to lay down their lives rather than yield to military barbarism.

St. Petersburg (Leningrad) was also the birthplace and home of Fyodor Dostoevsky. The novelist endured extremes of personal anguish and felt that suffering was the key to his redemption. One biographer wrote, "Dostoevsky kissed the cross with fever parched lips."

As a lad of eight Dostoevsky read the Book of Job in the Old Testament for the first time and wrestled for the remainder of his life with the tormenting questions it raises about human suffering and divine justice.

How did Dostoevsky suffer? He was an epileptic; he called it his "sacred disease." He was an inveterate gambler; he called this his "cursed vice." As a member of a revolutionary circle he was arrested and sentenced to death. He received a last-minute reprieve and was carted off to Siberia in chains. He was imprisoned for four years in a rat and vermin infested wooden building, unheated in the freezing winters and unbearably hot during the summers. Surrounded by thieves and murderers, he considered himself no better than the worst among them. When released he was forced to remain in Siberia where he married a deranged widow; she spent the night before their wedding day with a lover with whom she maintained an illicit relationship for years.

An observer wrote that his marriage was a "hell… a marital inferno, more than the cruelest imagination could conceive: a half insane invalid and an epileptic were torturing one another to death." When his beloved brother died he was saddled with his brother's debts as well as his own; it took him a lifetime to pay them off. A three-year-old son died because Dostoevsky could not afford to heat their living quarters. He walked the streets begging for money. Some say he was driven by "wild… explosive sex dynamics." He was a terribly disturbed man (and we think we have problems). The novelist Somerset Maugham said Dostoevsky was "vain, suspicious, quarrelsome, cringing, selfish, boastful, unreliable, inconsiderate, narrow and intolerant," and then added, "but that's not the whole story." The whole story included the facts that he conquered most of his inner demons before his death, became a devoted husband to his second wife, and was, in his own way, a profoundly spiritual man.

His novels, among the world's most powerful writings, influenced the fields of literature, religion and psychology. Freudians are indebted to him and Nietzsche wrote that he "was the only psychologist from whom I have anything to learn." He described the darker side of human nature, the frightening and inescapable burden of freedom, the cleansing power of suffering, and the reality of "a third something"—his definition of God. In his novel *Crime and Punishment* (1866), Raskolnikov, the young murderer, drops to his knees before Sonya, the prostitute who was a key to his salvation. He then stands and tearfully says, "I did not bow down to you, I bowed down to all the suffering of humanity."

If war represents a primary cause of mass suffering, Dostoevsky represents an intense personification of individual suffering. What can we learn from them?

From war? Its ultimate futility. World War I, "the war to end all wars," didn't fulfill its promise. World War II, "the war to save the world for democracy," didn't achieve its goal. True, the defeat of the Third Reich seemed absolutely necessary at the time. The Holocaust was one of the most tragic consequences of Hitler's madness.

VIKTOR FRANKL, A VIENNESE psychiatrist, was a Holocaust survivor. He has described one crucial night in his concentration camp. The prisoners were cold, weak and hungry; tempers were flaring. Suddenly the lights went out. The senior block warden, sensing the gravity of the situation, asked Frankl to talk to the men. Describing that dark night Frankl wrote:

> *I said even in this Europe in the sixth winter of the Second World War, our situation was not the most terrible we could think of. I said that each of us had to ask himself what irreplaceable losses he had suffered up to then. ...After all, we still had our bones intact.[7]*

He went on to talk about the future. In that particular camp the chances for survival were about one in twenty, but he had no intention of giving up. He talked about the past, "how its light shone even in the present darkness," and about life's meaning and the place of courage. And finally, he wrote:

> *I spoke of our sacrifice which had meaning in every case. It was the nature of this sacrifice that it should appear to be pointless in the normal world, the world of material success. But in reality our sacrifice did have meaning. Those of us who had any religious faith, I said frankly, could understand. ...The purpose of my words was to find a full meaning in our life, then and there, in that hut, and in that practically hopeless situation. ...When the electric bulb flared up again, I saw the miserable figures of my friends limping toward me to thank me with tears in their eyes.*[8]

Frankl explained why some of the prisoners stayed alive while most of them died in captivity. The difference? Those who stayed alive were determined to outlast their torment so they could return to their wives and loved ones, or complete unfinished projects, or defy their captors. They survived because of their stubborn, heroic resolve. Purpose made a vital difference!

We can suffer almost anything if we see that our experience has meaning beyond our seasons of pain or despair. Nietzsche rightly said that "he who has a why to live for can bear almost any how."

The suffering caused by war is incalculable. However, as Dostoevsky, Frankl and Nietzsche believed, based on their own experience, even the most excruciating human suffering can be redemptive. Sometimes our suffering, yours and mine, is as dire as theirs—more often it is not. Other maladies and setbacks invade our days: Chronic depression? Joblessness? Indebtedness? Illness? Betrayal? Crippling sense of hopelessness?

SOME YEARS AGO I attended a worship service that seemed to mirror so much of what we have been thinking about. It was in an African American church on a Maundy Thursday. The congregation was enthusiastic and demonstrative. The sermon was followed by the sacrament of Holy Communion. Then came a foot-washing ceremony based on the story found in the Gospel of John.

Sitting toward the front of the church was a gaunt, skinny, broken man. He was dying of AIDS and had not been in the church before. This was his grandmother's church, and she was sitting by his side. When the gospel songs were sung he stood and sang when he could. When the communion plates were passed he took the elements in trembling hands. When the time came for the foot-washing ceremony he arose unsteadily, went forward, sat on the altar steps and took off his shoes. A large motherly woman came down from the choir, sat beside him, and took off her shoes. They embraced. She knelt and washed his feet; then he washed hers. The congregation sang, "Were You There When They Crucified My Lord?" and, believe me, there wasn't a dry eye in the house. The entire experience was a snapshot of grace—desperate need, lowly service, utter humility, and love in action.

As I said at the outset, every one of us will experience hardship and suffering. A woman has a miscarriage. An elderly man falls and breaks a hip. A teen-ager loses control and fears she may be pregnant. A job is lost. A mortgage is foreclosed. You fall off the wagon. A baby dies. A youngster is killed in an auto accident. A loved one betrays you—the list goes on and on. We suffer, all of us suffer, painful emotional and physical loss. How we handle the pain and the loss is a fundamental measure of our potential for happiness and personal wholeness.

SO FAR IN THIS CHAPTER the stories told and incidents related are tearjerkers. We identify with those who suffer, or see ourselves as victims and try to cope with our own misfortune. Recently I read of a man who was dealing with mental illness in his family. He had lunch with a friend and asked if she could relate to his personal crisis. She told him of her boyfriend who had severe psychiatric problems that had put frightening strains on their relationship. She began to cry, and as she wept he realized that his own story "suddenly evaporated." He wrote:

> As I listened I had an out-of-ego experience. …My ego-self didn't matter to me. Only she mattered … she did something wonderful for me in sharing it. She snapped me out of my fixation on me, me, me: my fixation on my needs, my urges, grudges, ideas, plans, schemes… which fill up so much of my life but aren't the essence of my life at all… Her tears crucified my ego. The more often we can have what I call "an out-of-ego experience," the happier we'll be and the better life will be for others.[9]

The two people who shared lunch that day were profoundly "spiritual"— much as the Dalai Lama defined spirituality—and the woman referred to "a resurrected God, who is the loving, listening presence within me." The man who shared the experience wrote:

What would happen if I just let my emotional and spiritual guard down long enough to let my ego get crucified—so that it is no longer my self-idea of myself that lives, but the Christ, who is God, who is Love, that lives within me?

So that the eye with which I see God is the eye with which God sees me? So that I can be fully present and aware and delighted by the divinity that is your essence and mine!

Indeed, if we could let down our guard over our egos, it would be a "new earth" for us all.[10]

Some of you reading these words may not be comfortable with the Christ and God references. Go back to Fred Rogers who said that, "At the heart of the universe is a loving heart that continues to beat and that wants the best for every person." Most of the world's great religions would agree, and an other-centered humanism would agree. Grace is ultimate reality, and many of us draw strength and comfort from that firm belief.

Leo Tolstoy wrote a children's story about a tired swan. A formation of swans was making its rhythmic way across the night sky when one broke formation, lagged behind, stopped flapping its wings and plunged toward the ocean (think of those who are suffering among us). It settled on the tossing waves and looked up, but its companions "flew on without a backward glance." They became a thin white line streaked against the distant sky. The swan "curved back its neck and closed its tired eyes."

Tolstoy concluded the story:

(The swan) made no struggle: the sea rose and fell with its wide rolling waves and at dawn a light breeze ruffled its feathers and sprinkled glistening drops upon its pure white breast.

Its eyes opened. It stretched its neck, shook its wings as if reaching for the bluish dawn, and then tried to fly, its feet making a watery furrow along the surface of the sea.

And then, with a final thrust, it rose above the water.

Higher, ever higher, until at last it reached the open sky. And it flew on alone above the watery waves.[11]

A children's story. A metaphor. Our questions may not be answered. We may be tired—life-weary, bone-weary, soul-weary. But if we, like that swan, can find a second wind and rely on the natural ebb and flow of life forces, we may come to realize that "underneath are the everlasting arms" of Love. If we can wait in trust, until the dawn comes, we can resume our journey and fly on toward new horizons above the silvery waves. We don't have to have all the answers.

9

DARKNESS
AND DOUBT

9

I had known the man for more than fifty years. He grew up in a sleepy Southern town. He went to a small brick schoolhouse and a weather-beaten frame church. His parents taught him a simple piety. When he was in his teens a revival came to town and he was "saved" and decided to become a preacher. He went to school to prepare for the ministry, but with the passage of time he discovered that life was far more complicated, truth was far more illusive, and the good life was not nearly as simple as his parents and the evangelist had insisted. His sexuality confused him and his mind was filled with doubts. The emotional tang of his "conversion" wore off, and his determined efforts to make sense of things seemed futile. He wrote me, "No God I ever heard about could stand to see a person try so often, so long, without throwing him something besides little straws. If this is the nature of God, then I'm sick and tired of him and his damn haystack."

His brilliant mind turned away from religion and embraced an other-centered form of humanism. He moved from job to job, working with refugees in Europe and the down-and-out here at home. When Martin Luther King, Jr. was slain he decided to go to law school—he was president of his graduating class—and devote his career to the poor and the powerless. He did that, never making more than a few thousand dollars a year. Trying to cope with his inner demons and fearing his sexuality would be exposed—most gays of his generation felt they needed to remain in the closet—he drank too much and played too hard. With the passage of time he became a broken cynic, still trying to help people, yet unable to help himself.

We stayed in touch across the years. He called me more than once, toying with the idea of ending it all. Would God (if there is a God) forgive him? Would I forgive him? But he hung in there, clinging to some strands of hope. In his late seventies, he suffered from advanced dementia, bladder cancer and diabetes. With a mangy cat as his closest friend, he survived from day to day in a "senior living community." Not long ago, making an effort to find and form the right words and taking forever to get the words out, he said, "Jim, I don't believe in much of anything. There's no light at the end of the tunnel. It's all doubt and darkness." He returned to the town of his boyhood. He would sit on the porch of the assisted living facility that had become his home, rock back and forth in an old rocking chair, and filled with grief, pain and guilt, he would stare off into the distance and wonder.

"All doubt and darkness." A pitiful narrative? Yes. Sad waste? Yes. Unfulfilled promise? Yes. But, his name is Legion, and, although our lives may be radically different, many of us join him in fearing that darkness and doubt will speak the final words.

We may find solace in our religious faith. God, by whatever name we signify the transcendent source of our existence, is central to the lives of many of us.

ELIE WIESEL, LIKE VIKTOR FRANKL, is a Holocaust survivor. As a child he was packed into a cattle car with his family and herded by the Nazis into the concentration camp at Auschwitz. From Auschwitz they were moved to Buchenwald where his parents and younger sister died horrible deaths. When he was 19 years old and deathly ill, Buchenwald was liberated by the American forces. Writing about his release Wiesel described looking into a mirror for the first time. He wrote, "From the depths of the mirror a skeleton stared back at me. Nothing but skin and bones... It was in that instant that the will to live awakened within me."[12]

As a man of faith, Wiesel wondered how a just God could permit six million Jews to die in extermination camps. Indignantly, he hurled his questions against the sky. He has written, "I have never renounced my faith in God. I have risen against His justice, protested His silence, and sometimes His absence, but my anger rises up within faith, not outside it." We can wonder and question and doubt, but multitudes of us voice our doubts within the framework of faithfulness.

Whether we believe in much of anything or not, most of us are plagued by doubts. If we are thoughtful it is only natural that we raise questions. For instance: Why, in an orderly universe, would hurricanes and tropical storms like Katrina and Ike be permitted? Why, in 2004, was a tsunami allowed to ravage southern Asia, killing thousands of people and leaving hundreds of thousands homeless? What about earthquakes and other natural disasters? What about the insanity of war? The Holocaust? Hiroshima? Iraq? Why, during a decade that held such promise, were John F. Kennedy, Martin Luther King, Jr. and Bobby Kennedy murdered? How different the story of our country would be had they lived. And why did diphtheria claim the life of my older sister when she was an innocent child, and why did my friend in a sleepy Southern town have Alzheimer's?

Add your own list of unanswered questions. Even the Lord of the Christian faith screamed, "My God, my God, why have you forsaken me?" from his torturous cross. Why? Why? Why? "That's the oldest question asked... 'Why?' " mutters a character in one of Erich Maria Remarque's novels, "the question on which all science, all philosophy and all logic, have broken up 'til now." And, it will never be answered to our satisfaction. Does it follow then, that darkness necessarily follows doubt? No! As I have already suggested, we don't have to have all the answers.

Every one of us has entertained doubts. Some are monumental and some seem trivial. Is there a God, and why is my husband down in the dumps tonight? Is there life after death, and the Lions really do suck this year, don't they? Does life have meaning, and are these slacks right for me? What about the color? What about the waist? Things of cosmic importance and the stuff of every day. What are we to do with our doubts? Let's think about it.

Many people think that "agnosticism" is a dirty word. The fact is that most of us are agnostic. We simply acknowledge that some things are not knowable. Who among us thinks she knows everything there is to know? Maybe an occasional bullying boss or nagging mother-in-law, but most of us are wise enough to shrug and say "maybe" or "perhaps," or even "I don't know." If so, we are in good company.

Thomas Huxley, who first coined the word "agnostic" 150 years ago, wrote, "I (asked) myself whether I was an atheist, a theist, or a pantheist; a materialist or an idealist; a Christian or a freethinker..." He added, "Each group thought it had more or less successfully solved the problem of existence; while I was quite certain I had not, and had a pretty strong conviction that the problem was insoluble." Robert Ingersoll, who gained his fame and fortune by lecturing and writing about agnosticism, wrote, "Is there a God? I do not know. Is man immortal? I do not know. One thing I do know, and that is, that neither hope, nor fear, belief nor denial, can change the fact. It is as it is and will be as it must be."

Bertrand Russell, the British philosopher, confessed, "I ought to describe myself as an agnostic. Because I do not think there is a conclusive argument that there is not a God." At least he left some wiggle room for us.

Even Mother Teresa, the sainted Albanian nun who gave her life for the suffering poor of India, wrote a priest friend saying, "Darkness is such that I really do not see—neither with my mind or with my reason—the place for God in my soul is blank—There is no God in me—when the pain of longing is so great—I just long and long for God. ... The torture and pain I can't explain."[13] She also wrote, "Jesus has a very special love for you, but as for me, the silence and emptiness are so great, that I look and do not see—Listen and do not hear—the tongue moves (in prayer) but does not speak—I want you to pray for me—that I let him have (a) free hand."[14] Even as darkness and doubt engulfed her, she continued on with her noble mission in life.

QUESTION MARKS PUNCTUATE our lives. To deny the questions is to remain in the shallows, refusing to recognize and deal with the depths of our existence. We cannot know the truth in its fullness, but faith is "the evidence of things not seen." It extends reason as far as it will go and then moves beyond the realm of the provable. Paul Tillich, the famed German thinker who referred to faith as "a leap," once responded to a questioner, saying, "Faith embraces itself, and the doubt about itself." Edna St. Vincent Millay wrote, "Not Truth, but Faith it is that keeps the world alive."

Consider the faith of Elie Wiesel, the spirituality of the Dalai Lama or the prayer life of Gandhi, who, after being shot at point-blank range, muttered, "My God," and slumped to the ground. Think of the ultimate trust of a Nazarene carpenter, who, after shouting his "Whys?" moaned, "Father, into your hands I commend my spirit." A Jew, a Buddhist, a Hindu, and the cornerstone of the Christian faith: All embraced a reality beyond the here and now and exemplified the inspirational power of life lived for the sake of others.

So, how do we handle our doubts? We can sweep them under a nearby rug, but what good does that do? They still come back to haunt us. Or, we can embrace them, see them as essential stepping-stones toward a more meaningful faith, and harness our spiritual energies to some greater good beyond ourselves. Elizabeth Glaser, who lived only 47 short years, once said, "If I didn't have AIDS, if my life weren't so sad, I would be very fulfilled by what I'm doing. I'm realizing my highest potential right now."

To the very end Elizabeth Glaser tried to live life to the fullest, defying AIDS and continuing to function "in spite of." If Maya Angelou could survive her tortured childhood; if Lee Tai-Young could survive her imprisonment and humiliation; if Viktor Frankl and Elie Wiesel could survive their death camp experiences in the Third Reich; if Nelson Mandela could outlast his captors after spending more than a quarter of a century behind bars; if Mother Teresa, who gave her life to God, could agonize over His utter silence, His absence, and continue her servant ministries to the end—then who are we to turn our backs on those who need us and shrug off the challenge of tomorrow? Self-pity is not the answer. We need to refocus, reclaim the purposes and values that define us, and live and serve in the name and realm of grace.

10

OLDER AND GROWING

10

You've seen them. You've known them. Maybe you are one of them: those who are old before their time. They may be in their thirties, perhaps their forties. They have become couch potatoes, staring vacantly at their television sets for hours on end. They spend their days in meaningless pursuits. Their worlds have grown smaller and smaller. They spend less and less energy on creative endeavors. They are easily bored and have become increasingly boring. Regardless of their chronological age they seem to have grown old.

There are increasing numbers of people, however, who refuse to be defined by the number of candles on their birthday cakes. An article citing Warren Buffet (at age 77) and George Soros (at age 77) states, "In the corporate world, 80 is the new 50." Jane Fonda says, "I feel like I was born to be 70." Anna Quindlen writes, "Fifty is the new 35. You're not getting older, you're getting better." Barbara Walters, the pioneer journalist, who at the age of 80, told of a ring given her by the opera star Beverly Sills. Ms. Sills' husband had given her the ring engraved with the words, "I did that before." Walters says, "That is the way I feel. I do not want to climb any more mountains, (but) I am certainly not standing still." Research on aging is experiencing an explosion of interest as the population grays, people live longer and tens of millions of baby boomers enter their sixties. And many of us are not content to stand still.

In an essay titled "Growing Old or Older and Growing," the psychologist Carl Rogers traced his development between his 65th and 75th years. He acknowledged that there was some physical deterioration, with minor vision problems, arthritis and heart palpitations. But he could still carry his own luggage, was willing to run risks, conduct workshops, write books and articles, experience deep emotions, be open to new ideas, experience the same sexual interests he had at 35 (although he couldn't say the same about his "ability to perform"), and be open to new possibilities in the face of death. He wrote, "I believe that it is correct that I will never live to be old. …I believe that I will die young." He did manage to stay young, even as he drew his last breath at the age of 85 and moved into whatever the future held for him.

There is a famous painting by Goya that hangs in Madrid's Prado Museum. It shows a very old man leaning on a cane. The caption? "Aún aprendo" (I'm still learning).

As each of us is involved in the aging process, what do we need to be aware of? Open to? What do we need to learn? For one thing, while accepting the inevitability of the aging process, we can be grateful for lessons already learned, relationships maintained and blessed memories. One woman, looking back, said it:

Old age, I decided, is a gift. I am now, probably for the first time in my life, the person I have always wanted to be. [Many of us, reading these lines, won't be able to echo that sentiment.] Oh, not my body! I sometimes despair over my body – the cellulite, the wrinkles, the baggy eyes, the jiggly thighs and the sagging butt. And often I'm taken aback by the old lady who lives in my mirror, but I don't agonize over those things for long.

"I know I am sometimes forgetful. But there again, some of life is just as well forgotten and I eventually remember the important things. Sure, over the years my heart has been broken. How can your heart not break when you lose a loved one, or when a child suffers, or even when a beloved pet gets hit by a car. But broken hearts are what give us strength and understanding and compassion. A heart never broken is pristine and sterile and will never know the joy of being imperfect. I am so blessed to have lived long enough to have my hair turn gray, and to have my youthful laughs forever etched into deep grooves on my face. …I like being old but while I'm still here, I will not waste my time lamenting what could have been, or worrying about what will be. For the first time in my life I don't have to have a reason to do the things I want to do.[15]

Talk about "women's lib"! As that woman aged she was liberated. And after all that sage advice about jiggly thighs and sagging butts she added, "Some of life is just as well forgotten… [we] eventually remember the important things." So, what about remembering, forgiveness and forgetfulness?

As you well know, sometimes memory can be a cruel tyrant. A young mother was unfaithful to her husband. She broke off the relationship and tried to make amends within the family. She was filled with self-loathing.

When she came to see me she poured out her story. She put her head in her hands, sobbed, and muttered, over and over again, "I'm dirty. I'm dirty. I'm dirty." We met on several occasions. We talked about wiping the slate clean and starting over again. There was profound sorrow and genuine contrition. The prayer of the man in the shadows, "O God, be merciful to me a sinner," became her own. In religious terminology, she repented and found forgiveness.

FORGIVENESS IS never easy. There is no such thing as cheap grace. We can sing the old gospel song, "There's a wideness in God's mercy like the wideness of the sea," but remember—the cross is the central symbol of the Christian faith. One of the most oft quoted verses in the New Testament is, "God so loved the world that he gave his son." Whether you believe that Jesus "died for your sins" or not, the fact remains: whether human or divine, forgiveness is costly.

Have you ever been deeply offended or betrayed? Most of us have. A growing child does not live up to the promises she made. A guaranteed scholarship is withdrawn. A business partner makes off with the company's funds. A loving, committed partner finds solace, comfort, or simply cheap thrills, in the arms of another. Our children, who have said they would be there for us as we age, are not there when we need them most. How do we react? We cannot simply dismiss the sense of betrayal. We can't make light of it. But if we harbor feelings of resentment or rejection, the feelings fester, and, like a malignancy, they gnaw away at our innards, spread, and block opportunities for growth.

Only as we forgive can we recover our mental and spiritual health. And if we are the culprits, if we are the ones who have let significant others down, we will bear the burdens of our guilt, shackled by our unrelieved self-knowledge. To seek and experience forgiveness, or to extend heartfelt forgiveness to another, is an essential "learning." If we are, in fact, older and growing, we will embrace the truth of the universal prayer and forgive others even as they forgive us—and sometimes when they don't. To do otherwise is to stunt our growth.

Forgiveness is not easy. How does one go about this matter of forgiving others or oneself? There is more than one approach:

- We can empathize with the other and try our best to understand why the offender did what she did. What motivated her to be so hurtful and destructive?
- We can put the old adage to work and attempt to walk a mile in the other person's shoes to better understand his plight.
- We can look at what we perceive as another person's faults and confess that we, too, have flawed records. We may have done things equally blameworthy, or if not, we can at least acknowledge that we are capable of moral failure. "All we like sheep have gone astray."
- We can see the damage we are doing to ourselves. Resentment and vindictiveness are self-destructive. By forgiving either oneself or another I am liberated from the darkness of negative and judgmental emotions.

Forgiveness and forgetfulness may seem far removed from the aging process, but they are not. Unless we resolve our inner conflicts, the way will not be clear for us to move boldly and confidently into the future. Sometimes we are told to forgive and forget. Forgiving is one thing, forgetting is quite another. Some of our memories we need to blot out. I won't bother to recite a list of those sorts of memories, because to remember them is to drive them deeper into our psyches. It's the good memories, the transformational memories, that we need to revisit. Think of some of them.

What are your earliest warm and reassuring childhood memories? Do you remember your first day of school? Who was your favorite elementary school teacher? Mine was Ruth Meredith, my second-grade teacher. The year was 1932, George Washington's 200th birthday, and I was George Washington in a class play. I remember playing softball during recess time and hitting a home run that made all the difference. My first "girl friend" was Bonnie Mae Heller ("she had a feller; his name was Jimmie, but don't you tell 'er"— my first poem of note).

How about junior high or middle school? The puzzling, troublesome, mysterious onset of puberty? Your first, fumbling dates—or did they come later?

What about Campfire Girls, Cub Scouts, Girl Scouts, Y.M.C.A., overnight camps and sleepovers in the homes of friends?

High school? Football games? First loves? Sometimes they lasted, and sometimes they were heart breakers.

Courtship? Weddings? Honeymoons (blissful or something of a letdown)? College highlights? Career decisions? Moves to new towns and cities?

The armed services? I was in the Navy during World War II. My wife's father was a Marine officer. She grew up all over the place, from bases in Hawaii to North Carolina to Southern California, and joined the Navy during the Vietnam War. Her time in the Navy, the first time of her life she was "on her own," was a wonderful time of growth and newly gained independence. Sometimes fierce friendships, sealed during wartime, last a lifetime.

Think back and recapture something of the rapture, or at least the warm inspiration, of experiences at church camps or in religious settings.

There have surely been other highlights, some of recent vintage. Single them out. Think about them, and be grateful.

If we are truly older and growing, the growth can be stimulated by a healthy remembrance of things past. But memory is only one piece of a many-tiled mosaic.

A FEW TRUISMS ARE OBVIOUS if we are to continue to grow with the passage of years. We need to take care of our bodies. That requires physical exercise and healthy diets. I'll let you fill in the details on the basis of your own sets of circumstances. If you have physical limitations (e.g., crippling injuries) or health problems (e.g., diabetes or hypertension) you will adapt accordingly.

We need to take care of our bodies, and we need to continue to feed and challenge our minds. To what papers, magazines and journals do you subscribe? What books are you reading? Where is your curiosity taking you? I have a woman friend who is in her mid-fifties. An accountant with an MBA, she was so turned off by the 2000 presidential election that she enrolled in political science courses at a nearby university. She had grown weary of bean counting and would earn a second master's degree, this time in something she considered relevant. Acknowledging the fact that she might starve in the process, she was determined to start over again and do something more meaningful with her life. Only time will tell if she made the right decision, but she had the courage to continue growing.

Nelson Mandela is one of the truly remarkable statesmen of this or any age. He celebrated his 89th birthday with a group of notable friends including Desmond Tutu, Jimmy Carter and Kofi Annan. After everyone sang "Happy Birthday," he announced he was forming an innovative new group called The Elders. Speaking in a soft voice he said, "Together we will support courage where there is fear, foster agreements where there is conflict, and inspire hope where there is despair." His purpose was clearly defined, and, as always, his motives and demeanor were grace-filled.

Your dreams don't necessarily have to be that grand. Some years ago Fred Noble, a well-known north Florida attorney, went back to school when he was in his nineties and earned a degree in history. What did he plan to do with it? Who knows? But his mind was stimulated and alive as he soaked up a different kind of knowledge. Like the old man in Goya's painting, he was still learning.

It's altogether possible that you don't have the resources to cut yourself free and start over. Don't let that stop you. There are still libraries and museums to explore. And, as we suggested earlier, there are still new friends to make and new trips to take.

There are those who defy the odds and make headlines, like Grandma Moses, who started painting when she was 70 and became a world-renowned artist, or like Jeanne Louise Calment, who lived to be 122. She took up fencing when she was 85, still rode a bicycle at 100, and lived on her own until she was 110. We probably have neither the capacity nor the desire to emulate them, but at least they show us an indomitable will to stay alive while living.

Carl Rogers concluded his essay on "older and growing" on a delightfully hopeful note:

[As my 78th year] drew to a close, I was increasingly aware of my capacity for love, my sensuality, my sexuality. I have found myself fortunate in discovering and building relationships in which these needs can find expression. There has been pain and hurt, but also joy and depth.

The year was capped on January 8, 1980, when a large group of friends came to my home, bringing food, drinks, songs and surprises to celebrate my 78th birthday. It was a wild, wonderful, hilarious party—full of love, caring, fellowship, and happiness.

So I still feel I fit the second part of the title of this paper. I sense myself as older and growing.[16]

A friend of mine, Betsy Holloway, wrote a column for her local newspaper. On New Year's Day, 2000, she penned her wishes for the new millennium:

May we realize, as never before, the fragility of possessions, of family, of happiness, of life itself—and vow once more, and over and over again, to cherish each moment, to make the best use of each hour, to seize the day that will never come again.[17]

Betsy was 69 when she died of melanoma a few years ago. At the time her son, a doctor, said, "She lived by the philosophy, seize the day...*carpe diem.*"

Let me be very personal as I close out this chapter, just as I was in the chapter on contemplation and prayer. I am writing these words in my 85th year.

Physically, I'm in surprisingly good shape. My legs were shattered more than 50 years ago in a mountain climbing accident, so I walk with the aid of a cane (I use a wheelchair in museums and airports), but I can still walk. My bladder cancer has been in remission for more than a year. All other vital signs are as they should be. Exercise? I swim laps three or four times a week, and walk to and fro across the campus where I teach.

And my mind? How do I keep my faculties alert and working? Others will have to comment on that, but I try. I start each day by working crossword puzzles. Health authorities suggest that such mental activities help ward off senility, and even Alzheimer's. And since my retirement from the church's ministry, I have taught at a local college. My course offerings range from "Dostoevsky, the 'God-problem,' and Self-understanding" to "Ethics and Political Realism." When I retired I gave most of my library, consisting of books related to my "calling," to a nearby seminary and to younger friends. Since that time my library has been replenished with everything from existential humanism to political science. I can honestly say that I have read more and learned more over the past decade than during any comparable period of my life.

I retired in 1999, but that was a mere technicality. I'm still functioning as actively as age and opportunity permit.

WHAT DO YOU PROPOSE to do in your retirement? Oh, you can play golf (the exercise is good) or travel (as already suggested, travel is great) or you can simply vegetate and become a couch potato (there are no redeeming virtues in that option). By settling for any of these options we are denying ourselves worlds of satisfying and challenging opportunities. Health facilities, civic clubs and churches provide ample opportunities for volunteer service. There are philanthropies to support, hobbies to cultivate, good deeds to be done. So—volunteer, respond, cultivate, *do*! And that's not all...

In her New Year's column, my friend Betsy Holloway referred to relationships, to "family," to "cherishing each moment." I have been married three times and have three families with whom to relate. I not only have five children from my first marriage, but five stepchildren, and lots of grandchildren and great-grandchildren. We visit one another and phone and write—we stay in touch. In many respects we are closer now than ever before.

And, there is Sheri, twenty-five years younger than I—vibrant, doting and wonderfully alive. I identify with Carl Rogers when he speaks of "love… sensuality… and sexuality." Of course there has been "pain and hurt"—but, oh, the joy, as I cherish each moment and seize each day as a blessed gift.

"Aún aprendo"—and I'm still young.

11

ON DEATH AND DYING

11

All of us have attended funerals and memorial services. Have you ever wondered what people were thinking as they mourned their losses or celebrated the lives of friends and loved ones? How about the widow? Might she be remembering their good times? Their bad times? Was she remembering the affairs he had had? The other women? Perhaps she saw two of them in attendance. Why, how brazen could they be? What were they thinking about? We can imagine his widow was grateful for the good times—but also angry, confused and numb.

And what about the rest of us as we sat there, listening to the words and thinking our own thoughts? Would we want our service to be like this one? Who would be in attendance and what would they be thinking? What about the readings? The songs? And what about our partners sitting next to us? Which of us would outlive the other? What would our services be like? In such settings we come face to face with our own mortality.

"To everything there is a season, a time to be born and a time to die" (Ecclesiastes 3). That's a sobering but inescapable reality. How do we react? William Saroyan, the Armenian-American novelist and playwright, once said, "Everybody has got to die. But I have always believed an exception would be made in my case." It wasn't. He died at the age of 72. He was cremated with half his ashes buried in California, half in Armenia. We may ignore the fact, reject and deny the fact, or, like William Randolph Hearst, simply ask that the word "death" never be said in our presence—but the time will come when we will return to the ashes and dust from where we are said to have come.

Many of us are afraid of the Grim Reaper. A woman once came to my office to discuss her lack of faith; at least that was the pretext she used. She sat quietly for a few moments and then began to sob. Finally she muttered, "I'm afraid of death. I'm afraid to die." She had suffered a heart seizure after a minor automobile accident. The experience underscored the brevity and uncertainty of her life. Her husband was dependent upon her and she hadn't always been faithful to him. Her teenage son needed her and she felt she had not been a particularly good mother. She was deeply religious, but her faith was providing neither comfort nor hope. She suffered chest pains, a numbing sensation in her arm, dizziness, and she feared the imminence of death.

I saw her twice in the following weeks, but the once cheerful, confident, outgoing woman showed little progress. She continued to have her pains, experience her sense of guilt, read her Bible, pray her prayers and dread her death, all the while sinking further into depression. I referred her to a psychiatrist friend.

Some time later she came by my office. The psychiatrist had proved helpful and she seemed much better. She was working part time, for therapy, she said. There was an occasional smile. The tightness in her chest was gone. No longer was she avoiding crowds. "But I'm still afraid to die," she said. "I've worked through the 'guilt thing,' but I'm still scared to death of dying."

It may not be the moment of death that causes the dread, but what leads up to it: the lengthy illness, the possible pain and suffering, concern for our loved ones, the uncertain process as we approach "our final enemy." Paul Tillich once wrote, "The anxiety of death overshadows all concrete anxieties and gives them their ultimate seriousness."

THE PROSPECT OF DEATH often leads to a radical reappraisal of our lives. Lee Atwater was a controversial political strategist and something of a mentor to George W. Bush's "architect" and alter ego, Karl Rove. Born in 1951, he grew up and attended college in South Carolina. One summer he interned for the rabid segregationist Strom Thurmond. That summer refocused his energies and redirected his course. The South was being transformed, from a solid Democratic to a solid Republican stronghold, and young Atwater would become the foremost practitioner of the GOP's "Southern strategy." He specialized in "dirty tricks." His call to arms was, "Attack! Attack! Attack!" He savaged his opponents. As a consultant, his first major challenge was to help his candidate defeat a man named Turnipseed. He invented "independent pollsters" and used them to serve his purposes. He circulated a rumor that Turnipseed was a member of the NAACP—a kiss of death in the Carolinas of that day, and hinted that the candidate had been "hooked up to a jumper cable" (had undergone electric shock treatment). Turnipseed was defeated.

In 1980, Atwater joined President Reagan's staff. In 1988, he ran George H. W. Bush's campaign against Michael Dukakis, then governor of Massachusetts. When Atwater came on the scene Dukakis was sporting a 17 per cent lead in the polls. Shortly thereafter America was made acutely aware of an African American named Willie Horton. Horton, serving a life sentence for murder, was granted a weekend pass for good behavior (a Massachusetts policy), and while away from the prison, committed a robbery and raped a woman. Atwater promised to make "Willie Horton a household name across America," proving how inept and naïve Dukakis was. Willie Horton was featured in the political propaganda of the Bush campaign. The campaign also charged that Dukakis's wife had burned an American flag during the Vietnam War, and hinted that the governor had been treated for mental illness. Atwater said, "We'll strip the bark off that little c___s_____." Bush defeated Dukakis.

In 1990, while speaking at a fund-raiser for Texas Senator Phil Gramm, Atwater collapsed. He was diagnosed with a brain tumor and given only a short time to live. Confronted by his own mortality he "found God," became a Roman Catholic, prayed spontaneously with close friends, and offered a new quality of tenderness and love to his family. More than that, he called and wrote those he felt he had lied about and misrepresented, including Turnipseed and Dukakis, and asked for their forgiveness.

Lee Atwater attempted to atone for past sins. In the light of his checkered past, it was a commendable way to leave this life. Apparently his illness gave him a new set of values. He experienced a dramatic internal makeover.

But what about us? How will we deal with our inevitable demise?

Elizabeth Kübler-Ross wrote the classic, *On Death and Dying,* an insightful and penetrating masterwork that is required reading in most medical and nursing schools as well as graduate schools of religion and psychiatry. Once asked if our belief systems make a difference, she replied:

> *I was raised Protestant. In my heart I was Catholic, and I was made into a Jew. For 22 years I was a little bit of everything. Then I worked with dying patients and began to realize we're all the same. We're all the same human beings. We were all born the same way. We all die the same way, basically. The experience of death and after death is all the same. ...It all depends on how you have lived.*[18]

Randy Pausch was a computer science professor at Carnegie Mellon University in Pittsburgh. When only 47, he learned he had pancreatic cancer that had spread into his liver and he had only a few months to live. He was married to "the woman of (his) dreams" and had three young children. How could he prepare them and his friends? He gave a speech, a heartfelt and humorous "last lecture," to 400 colleagues, students and friends at Carnegie Mellon. He said:

> By speaking I knew I could put myself in a bottle that would one day wash up on the beach for my children, Dylon, Logan and Chloe. Here's what I want to share:
>
> Always have fun.
> Dream big.
> Ask for what you want.
> Dare to take a risk.
> Look for the best in everybody.
> Make time for what matters.
> Let kids be themselves.[19]

The professor became an overnight inspirational phenomenon. A video of his lecture appeared on the *Wall Street Journal's* Web site. He appeared on ABC's *Good Morning America*, the *CBS Evening News*, and *The Oprah Winfrey Show*. He co-authored a book, *The Last Lecture* (2008), and appeared with ABC's Diane Sawyer in an hour-long special.

One of the many persons inspired by Pausch was Nancy Gibbs, who wrote an article in *Time* about her father's death. She said, "The day I lost my father I found the gifts that grief can bring." She closed her article with these words: "Ten million people watch Professor Randy Pausch's Last Lecture on YouTube; see the shining, dying man; and quietly promise themselves to shift out of neutral, (and) stop being stupid about the stupid things. I celebrate Daddy's Deathday for who he was and what he made us, a day when gratitude came to life."

Shortly after his diagnosis, Pausch was heard to say, "We cannot change the cards we're dealt, just how we play the game." He appeared to agree with Kubler-Ross's emphasis upon one's quality of life.

Pausch's last lecture was prepared primarily for his children. We need to understand, difficult as it may be, that a dying person does have a responsibility to those about to be left behind.

Carl Adkins served as the colorful and courageous pastor of a large church in Mobile, Alabama, for 25 years. He was not your typical clergyman. A handsome, carefree redhead, he went to college on an athletic scholarship and earned twelve letters in four sports. In seminary some faculty members shook their heads and wondered about his suitability for any "holy call-ing." He arrived in Mobile driving a red convertible and promptly married a beautiful young debutante. Across the years, as the social conscience of the city, he espoused unpopular causes and influenced its power brokers, who found it impossible to dislike or resist him.

Stricken with a malignant growth, he was flown to New York City for surgery. He survived and was soon back discharging his pastoral duties and hobbling about his favorite golf course, inspiring all whose lives he touched. Then the pain returned—the cancer had spread, necessitating further sur-gery. Finally, he was told the cancer was terminal; there was no hope. He had tried to protect his family, but now his ordeal had to be shared. He wrote a college roommate and close friend saying:

> *The hard thing about it was I had to tell my little family again, the second time in less than two years, about my condition. However, they took it as you knew they would—like soldiers, and we have a covenant now that we will live one day at a time, making it as happy and glorious as possible. ... Each of the members of my family is aware of the fact that we have been trying for twenty-five years in this church to show people how to live, and now, we are going to try to show them how to die.*[20]

Some of us, like Carl Adkins, may approach death with a profound reli-ance on our religious faith. Claude Thompson was a professor of theology at the graduate school I attended. He was the second baseman on our softball team and I was the catcher when we captured the university championship. He was an athlete and outdoorsman. As a devoted family man and an ar-dent believer, he heard the frightening words "terminal malignancy" when he was barely sixty years of age. How did he react? As you might expect, with a sense of regret—he would be leaving a life he relished and a family he cherished—but also with a sense of keen anticipation. He wrote a widely circulated article, "How Do You Want to Die?" Quoting a definition of ex-istentialism, "I and thou, here and now, Wow!" He added that a vital faith "determines the way we live, not simply what has gone, not simply what is now, but in terms of what shall be... it is the certainty that tomorrow belongs to God."

Lee Atwater, Randy Pausch, Carl Adkins, Claude Thompson—each accept-ed the fact of his impending death and helped friends and loved ones cope with that reality and prepare for a future without him. Learning from women and men like them, let me suggest that you spend some meaningful time reflecting on how you can deal with your own mortality, and how you can accept and helpfully relate to the approaching end-of-life experiences of others.

IN THE OPENING PAGES of this book I introduced you to my mother, Frances Green Armstrong. During the final days of her life I visited her in a Southern California hospital. One afternoon I was holding her hand, and in the sacred stillness of the moment she turned toward me and said, "It's all right Jim, I have more friends over there waiting for me than I have here to say 'goodbye' to." It was a quiet, moving affirmation of faith.

However, there is a vast company of others who do not share that sense of assurance. Julian Barnes opens his book, *Nothing to Be Frightened Of* (2008), with the words, "I don't believe in God, but I miss Him." He echoes the mood of many agnostics, atheists and wandering seekers when he asks, "How can you be frightened of Nothing?" Death may come suddenly, as with an automobile accident or a cerebral hemorrhage, giving us little chance to prepare for its advent; or it may be a long, painful, dragged-out process. But it will come. Are we to simply shrug and surrender our lives to Nothing?

Barnes calls Christianity a "beautiful lie… a tragedy with a happy ending." He misses the faith he finds in Mozart's *Requiem* and the art of Donatello. He confesses, "I miss the God that inspired Italian painting and French stained glass, German music and English chapter houses, and those tumbledown heaps of stone on Celtic headlands which were once symbolic beacons in the darkness and the storm."

Nor does Barnes have much patience with "the secular modern heaven of self-fulfillment: the development of the personality, the relationships which help define us, the status-giving job… the accumulation of sexual exploits, the visits to the gym, the consumption of culture. It all adds up to happiness, doesn't it —doesn't it?" he asks. Then adds, "This is our chosen myth."

We have been thinking of living and dying with purpose and grace. There would appear to be little purpose and less grace in Barnes' logic. In a sense it boils down to Ernest Hemingway's "Nada." But remember, the troubled novelist blew his brains out. Believe me, there is more to life than Nothing.

There is purpose. There is grace.

Wernher von Braun, the physicist and astronautics engineer who helped thrust us into the Space Age, and Albert Schweitzer, the missionary doctor called by *Life* magazine the preeminent world citizen of the first half of the 20th century, once had a fascinating exchange about the nature of immortality. Ironically, it was von Braun, a vestryman in the Episcopal Church, who wore the mantle of Christian orthodoxy, insisting that we each face a day of judgment and will be held accountable for the lives we live and the faith we hold. It was Schweitzer, the saintly missionary, who confessed that we don't know; we cannot *know*. But, he added, we can trust an Ultimate Reality whose name is Love—eternity is in His hands.

Do you remember what Fred Rogers said?

> *At the heart of the universe is a loving heart that continues to beat and that wants the best for every person. Anything we can do to help foster the intellect and spirit and emotional growth of our fellow human beings—that is our job. Those of us who have that particular vision must continue against all odds.* **Life is for service.**[21]

So, we come to the end of our time together. We have considered a series of important ideas. You are a unique, free and responsible person. You have hidden depths you need to explore and rely upon. You will experience hardship and suffering. You will most certainly have doubts along the way. But you can cope with and learn from your suffering; you can move beyond your doubts.

As you live out your days, you will define your purpose as you nurture yourself and serve your fellow human beings. And, as a recipient of grace, you will embrace it, draw upon its resources, find yourself motivated by it, and reflect it in the activities and relationships of your life—today, tomorrow and through all the seasons of your unfolding future.

POSTSCRIPT

POSTSCRIPT

My grateful acknowledgments are many. First, to my wife Sheri, who patiently and carefully went over my manuscript with me. Her observations and suggestions were invaluable. To Tom Cook, a philosopher and Rollins colleague, who questioned many of my assumptions and made pointed and valid recommendations. To Stephen Swecker, my friend, editor and publisher, who did his best to keep me on track. And to George McGovern, a one of a kind—Robert Kennedy called him the most decent man in the U.S. Senate—political leader and humanitarian, who introduced this slender volume with a most generous personal word.

I first met George and Eleanor McGovern in Uppsala, Sweden, in 1968, at a meeting of the World Council of Churches. Later that year I became a bishop of The United Methodist Church and moved to South Dakota. The McGoverns became close friends. My daughter, Becky, served on his Washington staff and was married in the McGovern's District of Columbia home. Our lives intertwined across the years. As I conclude *Living and Dying with Purpose and Grace*, let me share with you two excerpts from their published writings.

In 1972, Senator McGovern was the Democratic candidate for the presidency of the United States. An outspoken opponent of the Vietnam War, he became a hero to millions of idealistic young Americans. He once wrote:

> *Those of you who are young must serve our society in order to preserve what is as old as humankind: the quest for justice, peace, freedom and dignity.*

And the Senator's loving wife, Eleanor, who died in January of 2007, wrote:

> *When I trace the inexorable forward movement of my life – the developing child, the coping mother, the growing wife – I see clearly there are no endings to the yearnings which move us, only new beginnings.*

SOURCES

SOURCES

1.   Maya Angelou, *I Know Why the Caged Bird Sings* (Random House, 1969). p. 24.

2.   George Carlin, from his stand-up comedy routine.

3.   Edwin McNeill Poteat, *Mandate to Humanity* (Abingdon, 1953). p. 76.

4.   Lincoln Barnett, *The Universe and Dr. Einstein* (Williams Sloane Associates, 1948).

5.   His Holiness The Dalai Lama, *Ethics for the New Millennium* (Putnam Books, 1999). p. 1.

6.   Fred Rogers, quoted in "Children Lose a Quiet, Honest Friend" by Robert Bianco, USA Today. February 28, 2003.

7.   Viktor E. Frankl, *Man's Search for Meaning* (Beacon Press, 1959). pp. 129, 130.

8.   Ibid., p. 132.

9.   Jim Burklo, "Musings" (tcpc.blogs.com/musings). June 8, 2008.

10. Ibid.

11. Leo Tolstoy, *Swan Stories* (Detlit, Moscow, 1980).

12. Elie Weisel, *Night* (Hill and Wang, 1960). p. 109.

13. Brian Kolodiejchuk (editor), *Mother Teresa: Come Be My Light: The Private Writings of the Saint of Calcutta* (New York: Doubleday, 2007). p. 1.

14. Ibid., p. 288.

15. Author unknown. Cited by numerous sources.

16. Carl Rogers, *A Way of Being* (Houghton Mifflin, 1980). p. 95.

17. Quoted by Tammi Wersinger, *The Orlando Sentinel.* March 27, 2008.

18. Elisabeth Kübler-Ross, *On Death and Dying* (Scribner, 1997). p. 121.

19. Randy Pausch, "The Lessons I'm Leaving Behind," Parade.com (www.parade.com). April 6, 2008.

20. Excerpted by permission from a personal letter from Carl Adkins to Dr. Henry Johnson, his college roommate and a member of my staff at Broadway United Methodist Church, Indianapolis, Indiana.

21. Fred Rogers, op. cit.

WORKS CITED

Julian Barnes, *Nothing to Be Frightened Of* (Knopf, 2008).

Fyodor Dostoevsky, *Crime and Punishment* (Vintage Books USA, 1866).

Sam Harris, *The End of Faith: Religion, Terror and the Future of Reason* (W.W. Norton and Company, 2004).

Bruce Marshall, *The World, the Flesh and Father Smith* (Houghton Mifflin Company, 1945).

Randy Pausch, *The Last Lecture* (Hyperion, 2008).

Adam Phillips, *Houdini's Box: The Art of Escape* (Pantheon, 2001).

Rick Warren, *The Purpose Driven Life* (Zondervan, 2002).

NOTES

NOTES

NOTES

NOTES

NOTES

NOTES

NOTES

RIDERGREEN
BOOK PUBLISHERS

ABOUT RIDER GREEN

A Fresh Approach to Book Publishing

Rider Green Book Publishers' mission is to give religious professionals, clergy and talented religious lay people their own publishing house. We help worthy writers successfully navigate the often bewildering world of book publishing. To do so, we use a business model that departs from traditional publishing houses, denominational presses, subsidy publishers and typical self-publishing services. Our goal is to publish quality books by religious professionals that benefit discerning readers and create opportunities for authors to succeed.

Rider Green respects the traditions of the world's great religions. We welcome queries and submissions on any topic or theme of general interest to an inquiring interfaith readership.

If you would like to learn more about what Rider Green can do for you, including a full range of publishing services at any stage of your book project, visit our web site at www.ridergreen.com or contact us at info@ridergreen.com. Or, you can give us a call at 207-457-5088 during normal business hours, Monday–Friday.

TO ORDER ADDITIONAL COPIES
OF THIS BOOK VISIT:
Http://www.jamesarmstrongbook.com

Made in the USA
Charleston, SC
28 April 2010